# THE DE SANTI
# CLOZE READING
# INVENTORY

◆◆◆◆◆◆◆◆◆◆◆◆◆

# The De Santi
# Cloze Reading Inventory

◆◆◆◆◆◆◆◆◆◆◆◆◆◆◆◆◆◆◆◆◆◆◆◆◆◆◆◆◆◆◆◆◆◆◆

by ROGER J. DE SANTI
*with Renee Michelet Casbergue
and Vicki Gallo Sullivan*

ALLYN AND BACON, INC.
*Boston   London   Sydney   Toronto*

**Library of Congress Cataloging-in-Publication Data**

De Santi, Roger J.
  The De Santi cloze reading inventory.

  Bibliography: pp. 135–136
  1. Reading—Ability testing.   2. Cloze procedure.
I. Casbergue, Renee Michelet.   II. Sullivan, Vicki
Gallo.   III. Title.
LB1050.3.D4   1986        428.4'076        85-22898
ISBN 0-205-08733-7


*Series Editor*: Susanne F. Canavan
*Production Coordinator*: Sandy Stanewick
*Editorial-production service*: Bywater Production Services
*Cover Coordinator*: Linda Dickinson


Printed in the United States of America

10  9  8  7  6  5  4  3  2  1      91  90  89  88  87  86

# Contents

◆◆◆◆

# Preface

◆◆

An individual's reading ability has a pervasive influence on virtually every educational setting. The purposes of this inventory are to identify individuals' reading abilities, their attendant strengths and weaknesses, and the difficulty level of materials most appropriate for instruction. This inventory allows the user to:

**PURPOSE**

- measure reading achievement
- determine the independent, instructional, and frustration reading levels
- diagnose an individual's reading strengths and weaknesses

The inventory is written for those who want to determine another's reading ability, preservice and inservice teachers enrolled in university courses, class-room teachers, assessment teachers, diagnosticians, and instructors in college developmental programs.

**AUDIENCE**

The inventory measures reading comprehension through the use of cloze passages. These are passages with blanks; where deletions were made, the reader is expected to insert a word in each blank. Word recognition and word identification are measured through the use of word lists. As a measure of reading comprehension, the cloze procedure was chosen because:

**APPROACH**

- It is commensurate with the view that reading is an interactive process between author and reader.
- It is based in silent reading, which is the predominant form of reading.

- Being based in connected discourse and requiring responses within the text while the text is being read, reading ability is assessed while the reader is reading.
- The cloze passages may be either group or individually administered without affecting procedures or standardization while saving great amounts of time.
- The time of administration is 30−45 minutes for an individual or a group and 8−12 minutes for scoring each individual.
- Passage dependency is enhanced as there is no information in addition to what is being read available in the form of questions and answers and no distinctive possible answer may be selected.

Reading at the word level can be measured in three ways through the use of the word lists:

1. Word recognition is measured with a brief time exposure of each word. As a result, it is quickly known whether or not a reader literally recognizes a word.
2. Word identification is measured with an untimed exposure of the words not recognized. This allows for determining whether or not the reader can figure out an unfamiliar word.
3. Word analysis skills are noted and summarized through the use of the Patterns of Word Identification sheet.

**ORGANI-ZATION**   The inventory is organized into six broad categories. The first category includes preparation and how to use, score, and interpret the cloze passages. The second category includes (a) the Sample Cloze Passages with their answer keys to allow for practice and becoming familiar with cloze, (b) the thirty Cloze Passages, and (c) the Cloze Passage Coding Form and Answer Keys to be used in the scoring and interpretation. The third category includes the twenty-eight Word Lists and the sheet for summarizing Patterns of Word Identification. The fourth category includes sheets for summarizing individual student performance, class grade levels, and instructional groups. The fifth category contains Technical Information related to the inventory. This section discusses the passage development guidelines, passage readability and grammar estimates, passage appeal ratings, and the results of field testing the inventory to establish its validity and reliabilty. The final category, the appendix scoring and interpreting exercises, includes student-completed passages with and without scoring and interpretation.

This inventory originated in my belief that it was possible to develop a theoretically sound measure of reading ability within the perspective of reading as a communicative process. The paramount purpose of such an inventory is to test comprehension in a way that is compatible with the primary mode of silent reading and capable of yielding both quantitative and qualitative information. It should also be time efficient, cost effective, and conform to the guidelines of test construction. The search for an existing measure yielded frustration. The completion of this project yields what I hope you will find to be a useful tool.

R.J.D.S.

# To the Reader

◆◆◆◆◆◆◆◆◆◆◆◆

If you are using the De Santi Cloze Reading Inventory for the first time, please take the time to follow the suggestions in this section to familiarize yourself with the inventory; this will require only a minimum of time and effort.

First preview the inventory; go through the table of contents; the sections on administration, scoring, and interpretation; the passages; the coding form; the graded word lists; and the summary sheets. Thoroughly reread the administration, scoring, and interpretation sections. Review the examples in these sections and compare them to the two examples of student-completed passages scored and interpreted in the appendix. Then score and interpret the two sample student-completed passages in the appendix (pp. 151–154).

Finally, administer the inventory to yourself. Select a passage (from the twelfth grade level), and make a copy of it and of the coding form. After you fill in each deletion in the passage, use the coding form to score and interpret your responses. (You can save time and paper by only making a copy of the coding form and writing your responses directly on it. This procedure, of course, is not recommended for administering the passages to others.) Refer to the scoring and interpretation sections or the scoring and interpretation summary boxes inside the front and back covers while you score and interpret your own performance.

Once you are comfortable with the inventory, review the time-saving suggestions in "Saving Time" (pp. 17–18), and keep the scoring and interpretation summary boxes handy for quick reference and review.

# Acknowledgments

◆◆◆◆◆◆◆◆◆◆◆◆◆◆◆◆◆◆

There are many persons whose efforts and contributions I wish to acknowledge.

Vicki Sullivan and Renee Casbergue joined the project as doctoral candidates and became collaborators and friends. The completion of their formal studies was a fulfillment of mutual desire and responsibility. Our collaboration and friendship has been highly valued and its continuation is hopefully anticipated.

Many people provided original writings before they were rewritten and edited. The efforts of Billie Andersson, Kathleen Arntz, Rosina Carbo, Renee Casbergue, Denise Clement, Deborah Danna, Carolyn C. Fitch, Lois A. Gerdes, Faye Giglio, Mary E. Guillory, Diann Harrington, Ann H. Laperouse, Evella LePage, Sheila A. London, Michael Martin, Marie Martorelli, Ann Nunn, John Paruka, Kathy Pons, Janet Clarke Richards, Lynn Silbernagel, D. M. Simms, Peggy Slavich, D. J. Smith, Vicki Gallo Sullivan, Jane P. Tesvich, Elaine Warriner, Cheryl Welch, and Leonardo Zambito are appreciated.

To the scores of teachers and thousands of students who participated in the field testing and data collection, my sincerest thanks. The results of their cooperation has substantially influenced the confidence with which this inventory is offered to other teachers and students.

Lisa Thomas, and especially Joe Autin, helped me laugh my way through learning that a mainframe does more than display the best picture in a gallery. Steve Zingraf's willingness to run through the design one more time (again) was a great help.

Kay Kelly never failed to type and retype correctly and on schedule. Beverly Anselmo consistently handled the many interferences which would have precluded attending to the task at hand. How each of these ladies maintains a core of efficiency within a sphere of apparent chaos is amazing.

To Sue, Lauren, and Hiram of Allyn and Bacon, I am appreciative for their substantiation of my opinion that people can, at the same time, be both businesslike and friendly.

Acknowledgments

# THE DE SANTI
# CLOZE READING
# INVENTORY

◆◆◆◆◆◆◆◆◆◆◆◆◆◆◆

# Introduction

◆◆◆◆◆◆◆◆◆

The cloze procedure was first introduced in 1897 as the Ebbinghaus Sentence Completion Method. It subsequently received attention in 1957 when Wilson Taylor proposed the use of cloze as a measure of the readability of reading material. During the ensuing time period, the cloze procedure has been the focal point of hundreds of studies and reports of many applications.

Cloze is based on the principles of information processing theory and Gestalt psychology. Information processing theory deals with the conceptual load that is transferred by a word itself and by that word in relation with the other words about it. Gestalt psychology deals with the tendency of a person's perceptions to automatically fill in a missing part such as the fourth side of a rectangle. When it is adapted to measuring reading ability, the De Santi Cloze Reading Inventory focuses on the interaction of the communication between an author and reader by deleting portions of the author's message and requesting the reader to fill in the deletions.

The purpose of this inventory is to measure the reader's reading comprehension, logical language production, ability to deal with the grammatical structures of printed language, word recognition, and word identification. The inventory may be used for screening, placement, and analysis of strengths and weaknesses. The administration, scoring, and interpretation of the passages offer many advantages. First, it may be administered either in groups or individually without affecting procedures or standardization and is, therefore, adaptable to the assessment needs of the instructional setting. Second, the inventory is efficient in that time consumption for administration is less than one class period, and after some familiarity has been acquired, it can be scored and interpreted in a short period of time. Third, being based in connected discourse and requiring responses within the text while the text is being read, reading ability is assessed while the reader is actually reading. Fourth, consideration of the reader's performance is based on silent reading, which, when appropriately implemented, is a primary goal of reading instruction. Finally, the inventory has no list of words or multiple choice questions from which the reader is to select the answer. As a result, it is more likely that readers will generate answers that are based on their actually reading and understanding the passage. Passage dependency, the likelihood that a reader's ability to answer comprehension questions about a passage is dependent upon having read the passage, is enhanced.

The inventory is made up of several components, and each is intended to help you fulfill the purposes of the inventory.

The Preparation section (page 5) should be consulted for information of passage identification and selection.

The Administration section (page 7) provides guidelines for administering the practice and examination passages.

The Scoring section (page 9) information should serve to both teach you how to use the inventory to evaluate reading ability and as a reference when scoring passages. The descriptions of the coding categories and their criteria are followed by Sample Codings of ten different Reader's Choices for the same deletion. Within the Interpretation section there are additional scoring examples to which diagnostic and instructional inferences have been added.

The Interpretation section (page 13) is intended to help you convert the information collected into meaningful and useful statements regarding an individual's reading and the direction in which instruction should proceed. Each interpretative value is described along with how it is derived. This section also includes examples of qualitative evaluations of Reader's Choices to deleted words and their diagnostic and instructional implications.

The information in the Saving Time section (page 17) is intended to help you become as efficient as possible in administering, scoring, and interpreting the inventory.

Although part of the inventory's regular course of events, please do not incorporate the time-saving suggestions until after you are thoroughly familiar with inventory and its procedures.

The Sample Passages and their answer keys begin on page 19. They are intended to develop the reader's familiarity with the cloze procedure process and provide an opportunity for discussing how content and context are important to the process. The use of the Sample Passages is discussed in the Preparation and Administration sections.

The thirty-six Cloze Passages begin on page 27. There are three passages for each grade level to provide for flexibility such as pretest, posttest, and alternate forms.

Beginning on page 89 there is a Coding Form and Answer Key for each passage. Each key contains the words that were deleted from its companion passage. The Coding Form is used as the basis of the Scoring and Interpretation.

The section about the Graded Word Lists begins on page 107 and the lists themselves begin on page 109. The ability to say the words in the lists is not a measure of reading ability. By combining both timed and untimed presentations, word list performance may be used to estimate the grade level of the passage to be administered, word recognition ability, word identification ability, and approximate overall reading level. This section concludes with a Patterns of Word Identification Sheet on page 123. The sheet is intended to facilitate the selection of instructional implications in developing a reader's word identification abilities.

The section beginning on page 125 contains three Summary Sheets. The first sheet helps organize the information about a single reader, while the second is for class-sized groups, and the third will help you organize instructional groups.

The Technical Information section relates the passage development guidelines, the readability and grammar estimates of the passages, the appeal ratings of the passages, and the validity and reliability criteria of the inventory.

The final section is an Appendix that may be used to gain competence with the use of the inventory.

# Preparation

◆◆◆◆◆◆◆◆

Preparations for administering the De Santi Cloze Reading Inventory (DCRI) include passage selection, duplicating passages, and a practice session for the readers.

Passage selection should be based on a passage appropriate to the grade level reflecting the performance ability or the grade placement of the reader. As the DCRI may be either group or individually administered, it may be necessary or desirable to select more than one passage for an administration session, since the abilities of students in each given grade may vary. If there is no information upon which to base passage selection, the graded word lists beginning on page 109 may be used to estimate the passage level to select. The word lists are also used to gather information regarding a reader's word identification and recognition abilities.

An alternate, and highly efficient, approach to getting started begins by giving a passage of the grade level that you feel comes closest to the level of the group as a whole. The passage is then scored in accordance with the guidelines provided on page 17 in the Saving Time section. For those readers who performed within the independent or frustration levels, a second administration can be planned with passages that are two grade levels above or below the grade level of the passage first administered. If you elect to administer a second passage, moving either up or down two grade levels will increase the likelihood that you will identify the reader's independent, instructional, and frustration levels.

In addition to its title, each passage is identified by a number followed by a letter. The number indicates the grade level of the passage. The letter tells the passage's place within a grade level: A equals first, C equals third. For example, the passage identified as 12C is at the twelfth grade level and is the third passage within the twelfth grade. Sample Passages are identified with a title, a number for grade level, and S for sample.

Having selected the Sample and Cloze Passages, duplicate enough copies of each, and review the following section about Administration. The information in the Administration section is for both practice sessions and test administration.

Preparation

# Administration

◆◆◆◆◆◆◆◆◆◆◆◆

A practice session should be conducted with the Sample Passage that is at the same level of difficulty as the test passage to be administered. The primary purpose of the practice session is to overcome the effects of unfamiliarity with the cloze procedure. When the Sample Passage is concluded, discussion of the cloze procedure should include the use of context and content to determine whether or not a word is a sensible choice for a particular deletion. Following the practice session and discussion, the test passage may be administered. If convenient, the practice session and administration may occur the same day. If several different Sample Passages are used in a single practice session, the amount of time for discussion may preclude both the practice session and test administration occurring the same class period. The amount of time for administration of a Cloze Passage with class-sized groups has been found to be 30 to 45 minutes.

The following set of directions should be used for both the Sample and the Cloze Passages. They should be read to the reader(s), and you may write them on the chalkboard for all to see. The directions are:

1.  Read the whole story *before* trying to fill in the blanks.
2.  Write only one word in each blank.
3.  Try to write a word in each blank. Guess if you do not know. You may skip hard blanks and come back to them when you have finished the rest.
4.  Spelling mistakes will not be marked wrong. Do the best you can.
5.  Please write neatly.
6.  The name of this story is _____. (Insert the name of the story. This must be modified if more than one passage is administered.)
7.  You will have enough time to finish.
8.  Do you have any questions?
9.  Please begin.

# Scoring

◆◆

Having administered the cloze passage, the reader's performance is entered onto the Cloze Passage Coding Form on pages 90 and 91. You may duplicate as many copies as necessary. Label the Coding Form with the identifying information of the reader's name, the passage number, the scorer's (your) name, and the date. As you continue to read this Scoring information section, refer to the Coding Form on pages 90-91 and the Sample Codings that are at the end of this section on page 11.

The Deletion Number (DN) column identifies one line in the Coding Form for each word deleted. The Word Deleted column provides space for each word deleted from the passage. Following the Cloze Passage Coding Form, beginning on page 26, there is an Answer Key for each passage. The appropriate Answer Key should be folded so that the list of words lines up with the Deletion Number and Word Deleted columns. The reader's response for each deleted word is transcribed from his/her Cloze Passage to the Reader's Choice column. The columns that follow are the Coding Categories that are used to evaluate each response.

The Coding Categories provide information regarding the reader's: (a) comprehension of the passage, (b) construction of logical statements that do not indicate comprehension of the passage, and (c) ability to deal with the syntax of the passage. As you read the description of each category, refer to the Sample Codings at the end of this section. There are additional samples in the Interpretation section. Note that for each Reader's Choice only one of the first five categories is checked and the last category may or may not be checked.

1.  The Blank Coding Category is checked if the reader chose no word for the deletion.
2.  The Exact Coding Category is the first of two categories that consider the reader's comprehension of the passage. This category is checked if the word

the reader chose is the same as the word that has been deleted. A misspelling or different grammatical form of a word is acceptable as long as it is apparent that the Reader's Choice is intended to be the same as the deleted word. This category should be checked even if a misspelling produces another form of the deleted word. Sample Codings two and three illustrate the coding of a properly spelled and a misspelled Reader's Choice where each is the same as the word deleted. Note that Sample Coding four may be coded as either *Exact* or *Semantic*. The process for deciding which is the proper coding is discussed within the Sample Codings.

3. The Consistent and Coextensive Meaning Coding Category (C&C) is the second of the two categories that consider the reader's comprehension of the passage. This category is checked if the word the reader chose is not the same as the deleted word, but is consistent with the author's message. Again, misspellings should not be considered as incorrect. If the response, although different from the deleted word, still maintains the meaning of the author's message, then a check should be placed in this category. Sample Codings five, six, and seven illustrate Reader's Choices that differ from the Word Deleted but still indicate that the reader comprehends the passage.

4. The Semantic Coding Category (SEM) considers the reader's construction of logical statements that do not indicate comprehension of the passage. Had the Reader's Choice indicated comprehension of the passage, a prior category would have been checked. This category credits the reader not for reading comprehension but for producing a logical statement. This category asks: If the entire sentence were read as the reader read it, could this response have made sense to the reader? Answering this question requires reading the sentence using all of the Reader's Choice responses in the sentence. This category takes the perspective of the reader and may be checked even though the meaning is different from what the author intended. Sample Coding eight illustrates that the Reader's Choice did not indicate comprehension of the passage but did form a sensible statement.

5. The None Coding Category is checked if none of the previous categories have been checked. A check in this category indicates that, from the viewpoint of logical language, the Reader's Choice does not form a sensible statement even independent of the passage. No credit has been given. This Coding Category is illustrated by Sample Codings nine and ten.

6. The Nonstandard Grammatical Structure Coding Category (NGS) is not related to the previous categories, which emphasized comprehension and logical language. This category focuses on the success with which the reader coped with the grammatical structures of the passage. This category must be considered for each response. The response should be considered as given by the reader in the entire sentence. In determining the coding, the whole sentence must be read with all of the Reader's Choice responses included. If there are two or more deletions in a particular sentence, the reader's response for each deletion is used when considering the grammatical acceptability of a single response. Check this category if the response is grammatically unacceptable. It makes no difference, when considering this category, if (a) the sentence made sense in light of the author's message, (b) the sentence made sense regardless of the author's message, or (c) the sentence made no sense at all. This Coding Category is illustrated by Sample Coding ten. Note that although both Sample Codings nine and ten were coded as being in the None Category, only number ten is also coded as Nonstandard Grammatical Structure. As discussed in the Interpretation section, this category may also be used to consider dialect and English as a second language responses.

For each response, there should be only one or two check marks entered on the coding form. There should be only one check between the Blank, Exact, Consistent and Coextensive, Semantic, and None Coding Categories. The presence of a second check mark is dependent upon whether or not the response is an example of a Nonstandard Grammatical Structure.

As examples of how the above scoring procedures are applied, a sentence from a passage might read, "The rabbit ate the lettuce." After being changed to the Cloze format, the same sentence could read, "The _____ ate the lettuce." The following sampling of possible responses would be coded as indicated and are those referred to above.

| Reader | Word Deleted | Reader's Choice | Blank | Exact | Cont Coex | Sem | None | NGS |
|--------|--------------|-----------------|-------|-------|-----------|-----|------|-----|
| 1 | rabbit | ——— | X | | | | | |
| 2 | rabbit | rabbit | | X | | | | |
| 3 | rabbit | rabit | | X | | | | |
| 4 | rabbit | rabbi | | ? | | ? | | |
| 5 | rabbit | bunny | | | X | | | |
| 6 | rabbit | hare | | | X | | | |
| 7 | rabbit | coney | | | X | | | |
| 8 | rabbit | horse | | | | X | | |
| 9 | rabbit | brick | | | | | X | |
| 10 | rabbit | run | | | | | X | X |

Reader one provided no response and the appropriate coding was, therefore, Blank.

Reader two provided a response identical to the Word Deleted and the appropriate coding was, therefore, Exact.

Reader three provided a response considered to be a misspelling of the Word Deleted and the appropriate coding was, therefore, Exact.

Reader four provided a response that could be considered as a misspelling of the Word Deleted or as a word different from the Word Deleted. Selection of the appropriate Coding Category should be based on your knowledge of the reader and which of the two possible words was most likely the reader's intention. When a scoring decision is doubtful, you should decide in favor of the reader. This benefit-of-the-doubt attitude should permeate all scoring decisions where uncertainty may arise.

Readers five, six, and seven each provided a response considered to maintain the author's message and the appropriate coding was, therefore, Consistent and Coextensive.

Reader eight provided a response that is not compatible with the author's message. However, when considered outside of the context of the author's intentions, it does constitute a logical statement. The appropriate coding is, therefore, Semantic.

Reader nine provided a response that contributed neither to understanding the author's message nor toward a logical statement. Even though the statement, as constructed by the reader, is nonsensical, the reader's response is as grammatically acceptable as the Word Deleted. The appropriate coding is, therefore, only the None Coding Category.

Reader ten provided a response that did not contribute to understanding the author's message, did not contribute toward a logical statement, and was not grammatically acceptable. The appropriate coding is, therefore, *both* None and Nonstandard Grammatical Structure.

Additional Sample Codings are included in the Interpretation section, which follows.

# Interpretation

◆◆◆◆◆◆◆◆◆◆◆

The results of scoring the reader's response to each of the deletions are grouped into interpretation categories that are representative of the view that reading is a language-based communicative process.

The interpretation begins by calculating the Total Number and the Total Percent for each of the Coding Categories. The Total Number for each category is calculated by adding together the number of check marks within a given Coding Category column. The Total Percent for each column is calculated by multiplying the column's Total Number by two (50 deletions × 2% each = 100%). All of the interpretations are based on the Total Percent for each of the Coding Categories.

The Traditional Comprehension value equals the Total Percent of the Exact Coding Category. A score of 58 percent or more indicates the independent level. This is the level at which the reader, without assistance, can understand materials of the same grade level of difficulty as that of the passage. A score of 44 to 56 percent indicates the instructional level of reading. The reader can understand materials of this level of difficulty provided there is assistance with vocabulary and conceptual development. A score of 42 percent or less indicates the frustration level. The reader should not be expected to deal with materials of this level of difficulty. The name of each level is used to indicate a reader's ability to deal with materials of a particular grade level. For example, a reader with an independent level of third grade, an instructional level of fourth grade, and a frustration level of fifth grade can read third-grade materials without help (independently); can read fourth-grade materials with the help (instruction) of a teacher, parent, peer, or sibling; and should not attempt fifth-grade materials, regardless of available assistance, because they are too difficult for success

*Traditional Comprehension*

(frustrating). The levels may be used to guide estimates of reading ability and materials selection.

**Total Comprehension**

The Total Comprehension value is derived by combining the Total Percent for the Exact and the Consistent and Coextensive Meaning Coding Categories. This value goes beyond the traditional comprehension value in attempting to identify the level of the reader's interaction with and understanding of the author's message. By combining these two, a truer picture of the reader's comprehension may be obtained. To the responses exactly the same as the author's words are added those responses that are consistent with the sense of the reader's interaction with the author's message. This value is interpreted on the scale of: 76 percent or more, independent level; 64 to 74 percent, instructional level; and 62 percent or less, frustration level. It is recommended that your decision to use the Traditional or Total Comprehension value, or both, be based on your purpose for administering the DCRI. For more formal purposes, such as program evaluation and achievement measurement, use of the Traditional Comprehension value is recommended. For more informal purposes, such as placement in instructional materials and assessment of a reader's strengths and weaknesses, use of the Total Comprehension value is recommended.

**Logical Language Usage**

The Logical Language Usage value considers the reader's ability to generate logical language structures. While the coding of the two previous categories was from the perspective of the author's message, this value evaluates the reader's responses solely from the viewpoint of the sentences that the reader has produced. The combining of the scores from this and the two previous coding categories does not provide a measure of comprehension. It does provide a qualitative assessment of whether or not a response makes sense within the limits of our language. To calculate the Logical Language Usage value, add the Total Percent for the Exact, Consistent and Coextensive Meaning, and Semantic Coding Categories.

**Structure of Language**

The Structure of Language value is calculated by subtracting from 100 percent the Total Percent for the Nonstandard Grammatical Structure Coding Category. The resulting value is indicative of the reader's ability to deal with the structure (syntax) of our language. This value is most useful if you look for patterns within the Nonstandard Grammatical Structure responses. Dependent upon the given reader, it may be beneficial to differentiate between those responses that appear to be dialectal in their origin and those that are not. This differentiation may be accomplished by dividing the Nonstandard Grammatical Structure Coding Category in two, one half for dialect and the second half for other grammatical codings. Similarly, responses from readers for whom English is a second language may be differentiated in this manner. While responses considered to originate in dialect or second language performance are scored the same as other responses, the division of the coding category can assist in interpreting the reader's abilities and diagnosing the reader's strengths and weaknesses.

**SAMPLE INTERPRE-TATIONS**

Presented here are diagnostic and remedial implications that can be drawn from readers' responses. Examples of nonexact responses representing those coded in each category are given to illustrate the types of qualitative evaluations that can be made based on readers' responses to deletions.

EXAMPLE:

When the public _____herd_____ of the abandoned Mary _____Celeste_____ , . . .
            (exact: heard)

If it is assumed that the reader really was thinking of a group of animals when "herd" was written, this response would be coded as None, and Nonstandard Grammatical Structure indicating that the reader derived no meaning from this sentence and could not follow the language structures used by the author. If most of the reader's other responses were appropriate within the context of the passage, however, it would be obvious that this reader did not intend the word "herd" to refer to a group of animals. Therefore, it could be assumed that the reader intended the word "heard," but simply confused the homonyms. This response, then, would be coded Exact, and the reader would receive full credit for comprehension.

Such a response would indicate that this reader had no difficulty understanding the message being communicated by the author. It would further indicate that the language structures constructed by the reader matched those of the author exactly in this instance. While the response does indicate that the reader may need practice with spelling to improve writing skills, it is in no way indicative of reading difficulty.

EXAMPLE 1:

The occupants _____of_____ the derelict ship had _____obviously_____ left it very quickly.                                        (exact: apparently)

This response would be coded Consistent and Coextensive Meaning, indicating that the reader fully understood the author's intended meaning and was able to reconstruct the sentence without altering meaning.

EXAMPLE 2:

_____Because_____ of the extremely superstitious _____nature_____ of sailors during that _____portion_____ of history . . .
(exact: period)

The inexact response supplied in this example would also be coded Consistent and Coextensive Meaning since the author's message was not significantly altered. Yet this response has more diagnostic implications than the first. While the basic meaning was retained, the word "portion" has different connotations than the word "period" and is less likely to be used to describe a time in history. Thus, while this reader has no real difficulty comprehending this text, a preponderance of such responses would indicate that discussions of more precise use of language within given contexts might prove beneficial to the overall language abilities of this reader. A better understanding of subtle differences in word meaning would both refine this reader's comprehension abilities and improve his/her writing skills.

Both examples are indicative of the fact that total comprehension is occurring. While some diagnostic implications have been discussed and suggestions have been made for possibly useful interventions, it must be realized that no intervention is necessary given those responses, if reading comprehension is what you are testing for.

EXAMPLE 1:

Yet the ship ___was___ in perfect condition, its ___anchor___ set and its cargo ___intact___ .

(exact: sails)

The response "anchor" would be coded as Semantic, since it deviates from the author's intended meaning, even though it makes sense to the reader. Such a response indicates that this reader is not paying careful attention to the context provided in the passage within which this deletion occurs. Because it was stated earlier in the paragraph that the ship was found "drifting aimlessly," it would be inconsistent to conclude that the ship's anchor was set.

This reader would benefit from lessons that called attention to the use of context within the text as an aid to comprehension. Such lessons, once internalized by the reader, would prevent the reader from making erroneous assumptions that cause inconsistent interpretations of the text.

EXAMPLE 2:

Yet the ship ___was___ in perfect condition, its ___engines___ set and its cargo ___intact___ .

(exact: sails)

This response would also be coded as Semantic, since it deviates from the author's meaning, yet produces a sentence with logical meaning. This response, however, indicates that this reader is having more serious difficulties with the text than the reader whose response is cited in example 1 because earlier in the paragraph the ship is referred to as a sailing ship.

This reader is also having difficulty attending to context, but that difficulty is probably due to a lack of appropriate background knowledge for interpreting this text. While the beginning of the passage clearly referred to "sailing vessels," this reader apparently did not realize that the vessels referred to in the passage did not have engines. This reader's experience with sailboats has probably been limited to modern vessels, which often do have motors to supplement the sails. Any knowledge of sailing vessels from the 1800s, however, would cause this reader to realize that the ship in the passage could not have had engines. The fact that this response was made indicates that this reader does not have enough knowledge about navigation during the 1800s or about the vessels used in that period of history to make an appropriate interpretation of the passage.

There are situations in which responses such as example 2 can be common. In these cases many readers within a group will write in responses such as "motor" and "speedometer." Thus, it could be concluded that the passage called for the use of background knowledge that many of the readers did not possess. If an examination of all the nonexact yet Semantic responses made by a reader reveals that most are due to a lack of background knowledge, then it can be concluded that the reader does not have reading problems so much as an inadequate experiential background in terms of the passage content.

EXAMPLE 1:

... the ship's occupants ___ghosts___ been spirited away into ___space___

(exact: had)

by an unidentified flying ___object___ .

A response such as "ghosts" instead of "had" indicates that this reader was not capable of using language logically to construct any meaning, especially not that intended by the author. Such a response would be coded as None, since no meaning was derived from this language structure.

This example indicates the most serious reading difficulty of any encountered thus far. It is obvious that, in this instance, a complete breakdown in comprehension had occurred. If this reader is relying on context at all, he/she is doing so in a disjointed fashion at the level of single words immediately surrounding the deletion only. Such might be the case if the response "ghosts" was prompted by the word "spirited."

Readers who frequently make responses that are coded as having no logical meaning would require intensive assistance before they could be expected to comprehend text at this level of difficulty. Such readers would first need to learn appropriate strategies to use when difficult text is encountered. They would benefit from lessons requiring them to make predictions about what they expect to read, after which they would read to confirm or discount those predictions. They might also benefit from the use of cloze activities in an instructional setting where appropriateness of responses in terms of semantic and syntactic considerations is explored. These, and many other types of activities that focus readers' attention on meaning, would help them to recognize that reading must include understanding the meaningful message communicated by an author.

EXAMPLE 2:

_____In_____ December of 1872, the _____ships_____ was found drifting . . .

(exact: ship)

*Responses Creating Nonstandard Grammatical Structures (NGS)*

The response "ships" for "ship," while coded Exact for its replication of the word used by the author in terms of meaning, would also be coded as Nonstandard Grammatical Structure. In this case, the reader created a sentence that violated the subject and verb agreement rules of Standard English.

The qualitative information yielded by an examination of this response is limited because the reader did create the exact meaning intended by the author. However, many such responses to cloze passage deletions would indicate that the reader did experience difficulty with the production of Standard English. This information could be important to a teacher who has set the production of Standard English as a goal for this reader. Thus, the DCRI Coding Category of Nonstandard Grammatical Structure can provide important information about readers' syntactic awareness.

In fairness to yourself and to the readers you will evaluate, please do not employ the following suggestions until after you have done six or eight DCRIs and have become familiar with the inventory.

**SAVING TIME**

These time-saving steps are meant to be part of the ordinary use of the DCRI. Once you are familiar with the DCRI, and have incorporated these steps, you should be able to score and interpret an individual's performance in six to ten minutes.

When scoring an individual, considerable time can be saved by not filling in the Reader's Choice column when the response will be coded as Exact. The general principle is to only write in misspellings and choices different from the Word Deleted.

When working with a group, additional time may be saved by scoring and interpreting only the Exact and Consistent and Coextensive Coding Categories and separating the group into the three performance subgroups of independent, instructional, and frustration levels for that passage. On the assumption that they will be able to do satisfactory work with the instructional materials being employed at the same grade level as the passage, both the independent and instructional subgroups are set aside until later. The coding forms in the frustration subgroup are then completely scored and interpreted with the intention of meeting their needs as soon as possible. The intention is not to ignore the class members in the independent and instructional groups, but rather to first provide for those with the greatest need. The independent and instructional groups' needs are provided for as soon as the frustration group has been tended to. The approach here is similar to medical triage where patients are sorted and allocated treatment according to a system of priorities designed to maximize the benefit of all.

# Sample Cloze Passages

◆◆◆◆◆◆◆◆◆◆◆◆◆◆◆◆◆◆◆◆◆◆◆◆◆

Dogs and cats are the most common pets for children. _____ are usually playful and
1
_____ animals. Children need to
2
_____ good care of their _____ . The
3                                    4
animals should have _____ of the right
5
kind _____ food. They also need
6
_____ water to drink. Sometimes
7
_____ pet will get sick _____ must
8                                 9
be taken to _____ animal doctor.
10
Children who want to have pets must make sure

that their pets get the right care.

The first time I spotted him, he was cowering in a brown box.

He looked small and _____ . His coat was soft
1
_____ glossy, and except for _____ speck of
2                                        3
white under _____ neck, totally black. He
4
_____ at me sadly as _____ reached for him,
5                                6
but _____ began licking my hand _____
7                                            8
wagging his tail when _____ picked him up. Soon,
9
_____ was running and barking happily as I played
10
with him. My puppy was the best birthday present I ever got.

## Form 5S
## Michelle's
## New Bike

Michelle loved her new bike. She _____ not wait to
1
get _____ from school to ride _____ . As she
2                                         3
guided her _____ through the front gate,
4
_____ was very careful not _____ scratch its
5                                      6
shiny finish.

_____ cool, crisp air and _____ ride up
7                                       8
the hill _____ Michelle's breath away. She
9
_____ along until the sun was setting and it was time
10
for dinner. Michelle could hardly wait to ride again.


## Form 6S
## Life on
## Other
## Planets

Have you ever wondered if there is intelligent life on other planets? Some
people have _____ to police that they _____ seen
1                                                2
unidentified flying objects. _____ have told stories of
3
_____ very strange sounds and _____ bright lights
4                                         5
in the _____ . But most scientists think _____ our
6                                                    7
planet is the _____ one in our solar _____ on
8                                                9
which there are _____ beings. No matter what you believe, it is
10
a very interesting subject.

Sample Cloze Passages

Have you ever thanked a squirrel for planting a tree? Although it may be hard

to imagine a four-legged, furry creature _____ great oaks,
                                              1
squirrels are _____ for planting many trees _____
                    2                                         3
our forests and backyards.

        _____ are famous for their _____ of nuts.
                4                                      5
Every fall _____ can be seen scurrying _____ the
                  6                                        7
trees and along _____ ground in search of _____ .
                      8                                       9
They may eat some _____ the nuts that they find, but they bury
                          10
the rest. Since the squirrels never dig up every nut they bury, many of the nuts

sprout the next spring.

Video games often provide hours of entertainment to those who play them.

When a coin _____ inserted into the slot, _____
                    1                                       2
silent silver screen bursts _____ life. Swirling lights flash
                                    3
_____ electronic buzzers beep and _____ . Tiny
      4                                              5
figures scamper across _____ screen enticing players to
                              6
_____ their abilities. If a _____ hits a target with
      7                                    8
_____ beam of light he _____ , it explodes into
      9                                  10
thousands of sparkling fragments. The player is then rewarded by electronic

chimes and the promise of a free game.

**Form 9S
Cheer-
leaders**

The life of a cheerleader is more than just exciting and glamorous.

_____ cheerleaders at most high_____ and
　　　　1　　　　　　　　　　　　　　　　　　　　2

colleges must maintain_____ grades in their studies
　　　　　　　　　　　　3

_____ are also obligated to_____daily practice
　　　　4　　　　　　　　　　　　　　　　　　5

sessions. In_____ to these responsibilities, cheerleaders,
　　　　　　　6

_____ student representatives of their_____ ,
　　　7　　　　　　　　　　　　　　　　　　　　　　　8

must conduct themselves in_____ appropriate manner at all
　　　　　　　　　　　　　　　9

_____ . There is a lot of work as well as fun involved in
　　10

being a cheerleader.

**Form 10S
Man's First
Walk on
the Moon**

On the lonely, lifeless landscape of the distant moon there sits an unusual,

intriguing vehicle. On one of_____ four legs there is
　　　　　　　　　　　　　　　1

_____ plaque, part of which_____ : "Here men
　　　2　　　　　　　　　　　　　　　　　3

from the_____ Earth first set foot_____ the
　　　　　　4　　　　　　　　　　　　　　　　5

moon." This vehicle_____ the lower portion of
　　　　　　　　　　6

_____ lunar landing craft, a_____ to the extra-
　　　7　　　　　　　　　　　　　　　　　8

ordinary moment_____ two American astronauts imprinted
　　　　　　　　　9

_____ very first human footsteps on the moon's surface.
　　10

They set up a television camera so that the whole world could view the

historic event, and instantly became heroes of the nation and the world.

Sample Cloze Passages

Byron wished that the plane ride would hurry up and end. It

_____ a bumpy, uncomfortable four _____ flight
    1                                              2
and the jet_____ and dipped as it _____ through
              3                              4
the menacing clouds. _____ passengers were already airsick,
                           5

_____ were just very tense_____ a few actually
      6                               7
appeared _____ be enjoying the adventure. _____
               8                                        9
stewardesses were kept very _____ as they tried to soothe
                                  10
nervous people and help the sick. Byron suddenly felt a strange feeling in his

stomach and knew that he would be needing help also.

Have you ever applied for a job and felt that you were not even being

considered for the position? If so, perhaps _____ should
                                                      1
consider the image_____ projected when applying for
                          2

_____ position. The majority of_____ are seeking
      3                                      4
someone who _____ to be enthusiastic and_____
                   5                                       6
to be interested in _____ business. Additionally, many
                          7
employers _____ someone who is interested _____
                 8                                        9
a future with their _____ , not someone who will resign in a few
                          10
months. Keeping these things in mind when you prepare for an interview

should improve your chances of acquiring the job you desire.

Form 12S
Improving
Your
Chances
of Getting
a Job

186002

**3S**
1. they
2. friendly
3. take
4. pets
5. plenty
6. of
7. enough
8. a
9. and
10. the

**4S**
1. frightened
2. and
3. a
4. his
5. looked
6. I
7. he
8. and
9. I
10. he

**5S**
1. could
2. home
3. it
4. way
5. she
6. to
7. the
8. the
9. took
10. rode

**6S**
1. reported
2. have
3. others
4. hearing
5. seeing
6. sky
7. that
8. only
9. system
10. intelligent

**7S**
1. planting
2. known
3. in
4. they
5. burying
6. they
7. among
8. the
9. nuts
10. of

**8S**
1. is
2. the
3. into
4. and
5. ring
6. the
7. test
8. player
9. the
10. controls

**9S**
1. the
2. schools
3. good
4. and
5. attend
6. addition
7. the
8. schools
9. an
10. times

**10S**
1. its
2. a
3. reads
4. planet
5. upon
6. is
7. the
8. monument
9. when
10. the

**11S**
1. was
2. hour
3. bounced
4. flew
5. many
6. and
7. although
8. to
9. the
10. busy

**12S**
1. you
2. you
3. the
4. employers
5. seems
6. appears
7. the
8. seek
9. in
10. company

# Cloze Passages
◆◆◆◆◆◆◆◆◆◆◆◆

# Form 3A  The Four Seasons and What Each Brings

READER'S NAME _____

There are four seasons in a year: winter, spring, summer,

and fall. There _____ something special and unique
_____1_____

_____ each season.
___2___

    In winter _____ is very cold. Making _____ ,
_____3_____              4

ice skating, and snowball _____ are all part of
_____5_____

_____ winter season where there _____ snow.
___6___                     7

Some places never _____ snow but it still _____
_____8_____          9

very cold. Basketball is _____ winter sport because it
_____10_____

_____ be played indoors. Winter _____ a time for
___11___                  12

coats, _____ and mittens.
___13___

    When it _____ warming up, winter is _____ .
_____14_____             15

Spring has arrived when _____ and trees start getting
_____16_____

_____ leaves. The weather is _____ right for
___17___              18

playing outdoor _____ such as baseball. All
_____19_____

_____ the animals come out _____ their winter
___20___             21

homes. Baby _____ hatch out of their _____ and
_____22_____          23

caterpillars keep busy _____ new green leaves.
_____24_____

Summer _____ spring. Bees and butterflies
                25
_____ on the flowers which _____ blooming
      26                                              27
everywhere. Summer days _____ hot and very long.
                                         28
_____ is a good time _____ swimming, playing
      29                                    30
tennis, and _____ on picnics.
                  31
   When the _____ begin to drop off _____ the
                  32                                        33
trees the fall _____ come. The leaves turn _____
                     34                                          35
different colors. The days _____ cool. Animals begin to
                                    36
_____ ready for winter. Squirrels _____ to
      37                                              38
gather nuts and _____ birds prepare to fly _____ .
                        39                                        40
Turtles, toads, and frogs _____ themselves in the mud
                                 41
_____ the bottom of ponds _____ ditches. Foot-
      42                                         43
ball is a _____ sport. Fall is good _____ weather
                44                                    45
because the temperature _____ not too hot or
                                    46
_____ cold. When Winter returns _____ yearly
      47                                              48
cycle is complete. _____ changing of seasons will
                          49
_____ begin all over again. Winter, spring, summer,
      50
and fall are all wonderful times of the year.

# Form 3B  A Boy's Wish Come True

READER'S NAME _____

James was a boy who dreamed of owning a pony. His parents

had explained to him that he could not _____ a pony in
<br>1

the _____ . His family lived in _____ apartment
<br>2           3

and there was _____ place near to keep _____
<br>      4             5

pony. This made the _____ very unhappy. He still
<br>        6

_____ of ponies.
<br> 7

  Each time _____ heard of a fair _____
<br>       8          9

included pony rides, he _____ beg his mother to
<br>          10

_____ him. James would spend _____ entire day
<br> 11             12

riding on _____ ponies. He thought it _____ be
<br>    13            14

such fun to _____ his own. He dreamed _____
<br>    15            16

feeding his pony oats _____ hay. As a special
<br>       17

_____ , James would give him _____ of sugar.
<br> 18             19

  One day _____ father returned from work
<br>      20

_____ the announcement that the _____ would
<br> 21             22

be moving to _____ country. James's father had
<br>     23

_____ 24 _____ a new and better _____ 25 _____ . The boy was very

_____ 26 _____ . He did not want _____ 27 _____ leave his friends

and _____ 28 _____ a new school. This _____ 29 _____ him

very much.

A _____ 30 _____ months later his family _____ 31 _____ to the

country. James _____ 32 _____ at a new school _____ 33 _____ was

a long distance _____ 34 _____ his home. He had _____ 35 _____

walk two miles to _____ 36 _____ every day. The boy _____ 37 _____

new friends, but he _____ 38 _____ still sad. His new

_____ 39 _____ did not live close _____ 40 _____ his home and he

_____ 41 _____ often lonely.

His parents _____ 42 _____ the situation. They were

_____ 43 _____ living in the country _____ 44 _____ there was no

reason _____ 45 _____ James not having a _____ 46 _____ any-

more. They decided to _____ 47 _____ the pony for his

_____ 48 _____ . It would be a _____ 49 _____ .

On the morning of _____ 50 _____ birthday, his mother and

father gave him the pony. It was the happiest birthday that

James had ever had.

## Form 3C  Koala Bears

Koalas look like teddy bears, but they are not bears at all.

They _____ really animals called marsupials.
       1

_____ animals carry their young _____ pouches,
  2                                   3

like kangaroos do.

_____ live in the forests _____ Australia.
    4                            5

They spend most _____ their lives in eucalyptus
                      6

_____ . They hardly ever come _____ even for a
  7                              8

drink _____ water. In fact, their _____ means
         9                      10

"no drink." The _____ have a way of _____ which
              11                  12

trees they can _____ on safely. They eat _____
              13                    14

leaf the same way. _____ , they bite the leaf
                15

_____ the stem and then _____ chew it from
  16                    17

base _____ tip.
     18

When a koala _____ born, it is less _____ an
                  19                  20

inch long. The _____ crawls into the mother's
              21

_____ right away and stays _____ for six
  22                      23

months. After _____ , the baby rides piggyback
             24

_____ hangs on between the _____ front paws
25                                                                              26

and legs. _____ koalas stay with their _____ for
27                                                                     28

at least a _____ .
29

   The koala is a _____ climber. Its paws end
30

_____ sharp claws, so he _____ get a good grip
31                                                          32

_____ tree branches. Koalas sleep _____ the
33                                                                      34

eucalyptus trees through _____ of the day and
35

_____ at night. Koalas may _____ alone or in
36                                                          37

small _____ . Males sometimes use their _____
38                                                                              39

claws as weapons. Most _____ the time, koala families
40

_____ together peacefully.
41

   Most zoos _____ it hard to take _____ care of
42                                                          43

koala bears. _____ San Diego Zoo is _____ only
44                                                          45

place outside Australia _____ people can see the
46

_____ . Many people go to _____ zoo to see the
47                                                          48

_____ . The animal is beloved _____ people,
49                                                          50

because of the sweet look on its face. Some koalas are not

even afraid of people and like to hug them.

# Form 4A  The Big Campout

READER'S NAME _____

Paul and his sister, Susan, excitedly rolled out their sleeping bags on the floor of

the tent. This was _____ to be their first _____ . They had
                          1                              2

spent the _____ afternoon gathering the supplies _____
                  3                                              4

would need.

    Susan brought _____ radio so they could _____ to the
                              5                              6

weather reports. _____ planned to dig a _____ around the
                        7                              8

tent to _____ it from flooding if _____ rained. And both of
                9                              10

_____ had two sets of _____ clothes just in case
      11                              12

_____ got wet or dirty.
      13

    _____ insisted that they each _____ to have a flashlight.
            14                              15

_____ pointed out that they _____ need them to keep
      16                              17

_____ tripping over the roots _____ trees if they had
      18                              19

_____ leave the tent in _____ middle of the night.
      20                              21

    _____ was Susan who thought _____ bringing whistles
            22                              23

for both _____ them. She was pretty _____ that they could
                24                              25

make _____ noise with the whistles _____ scare off any wild
          26                              27

_____ that might wander into _____ camp. And if that
      28                              29

_____ work, the whistles could _____ heard far enough away
      30                              31

_____ call for help. The _____ could also be used
      32                              33

_____ help them find each _____ if they became separated.
      34                              35

Copyright © 1986 by Allyn and Bacon, Inc. Use of this material is restricted to duplication from this master.

Cloze Passages          35

_____ 36 _____ , Paul and Susan had _____ 37 _____ a place for these _____ 38 _____ all their other supplies. _____ 39 _____ settled down to read _____ 40 _____ comic books, using their _____ 41 _____ to see the pages. _____ 42 _____ Paul suddenly realized that _____ 43 _____ had forgotten the most _____ 44 _____ supplies! They didn't have _____ 45 _____ snack foods! He looked _____ 46 _____ Susan, and she nodded _____ 47 _____ head. They knew what _____ 48 _____ had to do. They _____ 49 _____ the flaps to the _____ 50 _____ and sped across the yard and into the kitchen. There they found cookies and milk waiting for them on the table.

Cloze Passages

# Form 4B  The Amazing Circus

READER'S NAME _____

Going to the circus is fun. There are lots _____ interesting people and

animals _____ tricks that are truly _____ .
           2                                   3

1

If you watch the _____ tamer in the cage _____ several
                        4                           5

big cats at _____ time, it is thrilling. _____ you hear the
              6                            7

tigers _____ lions roar, you wonder _____ they are ready t •
        8                                9

_____ their master. But soon _____ discover that the
   10                             11

ferocious _____ are just part of _____ show.
          12                     13

You can see _____ doing a variety of _____ at the circus.
         14                         15

They _____ on their hind paws _____ balance balls on their
      16                           17

_____ . We wish we could _____ our dogs to sit
   18                          19

_____ come upon our command.
   20

_____ is always amazing that _____ juggler can handle
   21                            22

so _____ balls or other objects _____ his hands at one
      23                         24

_____ . But many jugglers even _____ their feet and heads
   25                          26

_____ their acts.
   27

The juggler _____ to be quick, but _____ magician has to
          28                        29

be _____ faster to fool the _____ . You can see elephants
     30                         31

_____ cars disappear before your _____ . And no matter how
   32                         33

_____ you try you cannot _____ how these tricks are
   34                        35

_____ .
   36

You might find yourself _____ your breath as you _____
        37                                              38
the acrobats flying through _____ air from one swing _____
                           39                                    40
the other. And it _____ thrilling to watch the _____ rope
                  41                                   42
walker balance on _____ narrow rope.
                  43

  You can _____ all the way through _____ circus because
          44                                45
there are _____ clowns nearby doing silly _____ . It is
          46                                     47
surprising that _____ are never hurt when _____ hit each
                48                                 49
other and _____ over their own big feet.
          50
It is fun to see all of these entertaining people and animals at the circus.

# Form 4C  Reptiles

READER'S NAME _____

Reptiles are strange and beautiful animals. Reptiles _____ bodies that

 1

are covered _____ small scales. Lizards and _____ are

 2  3

reptiles. Alligators, crocodiles, _____ turtles are reptiles, too.

 4

_____ have very long tails. _____ an enemy grabs one

 5  6

_____ the tail, it snaps _____ . The lizard runs away.

 7  8

_____ it will grow a _____ tail.

 9  10

Snakes are interesting _____ . Some snakes are harmless

 11

_____ cannot hurt you. Some _____ are very poisonous. They

 12  13

_____ fangs which are like _____ , hollow teeth. When these

 14  15

_____ bite, the fangs fill _____ poison which can kill

 16  17

_____ animals and people too.

 18

_____ catch fish in their _____ jaws. These reptiles

 19  20

spend _____ of their lives in _____ water. Most people have

 21  22

_____ telling the difference between _____ alligator and

 23  24

another reptile _____ the crocodile. The alligator _____ a

 25  26

broad, fat snout _____ likes swamps. The crocodile _____ a

 27  28

long, sharp snout.

_____ interesting reptile is the _____ . All turtles hatch

 29  30

from _____ . The mother turtle comes _____ of the water to

 31  32

_____ her eggs on the _____ . As soon as the _____
33                                    34                              35

turtles hatch, they hurry _____ the beach to their _____ in
36                                    37

the sea.

      Some _____ are small; others are _____ large. Some
38                                    39

have scales _____ bright colors and are _____ to see. Others
40                                    41

are _____ to see because they _____ their surroundings.
42                                    43

Some reptiles _____ helpful to man. Some _____ harmful to
44                                    45

man. If _____ are not familiar with _____ , you should visit
46                                    47

your _____ zoo. Reptiles are strange, _____ creatures. They
48                                    49

are all _____ of our world of nature. Studying about reptiles can be fun.
50

# Form 5A  A Frightening Canoe Trip

READER'S NAME  _____

The canoe skimmed swiftly through the water, and at last the boys were on their

way. Tom could see his _____ wave in the distance, _____ ,

               1                                                2

and walk back to _____ car. Dad would meet _____ sons in

                     3                                         4

the village _____ Indian Gulch tomorrow afternoon. _____

               5                                           6

was Tom's first canoe _____ without his father, but _____

                   7                                        8

was not afraid because _____ older brother Josh was _____

                   9                                      10

him. Tom figured Josh _____ handle anything that came

                   11

_____ .

   12

    The warmth of the _____ made them shed their _____ by

                     13                                       14

noon. A few _____ clouds floated across the _____ sky.

               15                                    16

Around them, the _____ of the forest was _____ only by the

                   17                                 18

occasional _____ of birds. The canoe _____ effortlessly, and

             19                                   20

Tom settled _____ to imagine what the _____ had been like

                   21                                 22

before _____ white men arrived.

       23

    Suddenly _____ was jolted out of _____ daydream. The

                 24                                 25

canoe was _____ and twisting, and Josh _____ yelling. Their

            26                                 27

canoe, out _____ control, had taken the _____ stream and

            28                                 29

had hit _____ rapids. Tom could barely _____ Josh above the

          30                                 31

roar _____ the swirling water. Tom _____ hard to the right

      32                                     33

_____ 34 _____ head them away from _____ 35 _____ rocks, but his paddle
_____ 36 _____ jerked out of his _____ 37 _____ . Sadly, he watched it
_____ 38 _____ along in front of _____ 39 _____ . Josh shouted again to
_____ 40 _____ on tight, and Tom _____ 41 _____ see they had no
_____ 42 _____ choice. The chilly water _____ 43 _____ at their faces, and
_____ 44 _____ their clothes were drenched. _____ 45 _____ expected that any
minute _____ 46 _____ canoe would be flipped _____ 47 _____ , and they'd be
swimming _____ 48 _____ their lives.

  All at _____ 49 _____ they became aware of _____ 50 _____ calm around
them as they realized that the churning, bubbling white water was behind them.

They somehow had made it.

# Form 5B  The Truth about Dinosaurs

READER'S NAME _____

Some movies have been made in which cavemen are threatened by hungry

dinosaurs. _____ these movies may be _____ , they do not
              1                                      2

give _____ true picture of dinosaurs. _____ have found that
        3                                     4

these _____ died out long before _____ lived on this earth.
        5                                  6

_____ ideas about dinosaurs have _____ proven wrong
        7                                  8

by scientists. _____ many movies, the dinosaurs _____
              9                                10

shown as huge killers _____ long necks and tails. _____ legs
                11                            12

are often the _____ of tree trunks.
            13

Some _____ these creatures did exist. _____ dinosaurs,
           14                          15

however, did not _____ like that. Some were _____ size of
            16                          17

dogs today. _____ did not even eat _____ . They fed off of
          18                          19

_____ native to their environment. _____ that did eat meat
    20                              21

_____ stalked and killed animals _____ their food. Instead
    22                              23

they _____ the remains of animals _____ killed and partly
       24                            25

eaten _____ other dinosaurs. Not all _____ looked like
       26                            27

overgrown lizards _____ . Some had no tails. _____
            28                          29

resembled large birds with _____ wings and beaks.
                  30

Some _____ seemed to have a _____ mixture of both bird
           31                          32

_____ reptile features. One such _____ was the duckbill, an
    33                              34

_____ creature whose short and _____ body caused it to
    35                                 36

_____ when it walked. Despite _____ size, the duckbill was
    37                                 38

_____ harmless, eating only plants _____ fruit. Its strangest
    39                                 40

feature _____ a large, flat snout _____ looked like a duck's
           41                          42

_____ , thus giving this creature _____ name.
    43                                 44

    Scientific findings proving _____ such odd dinosaurs as
                           45

_____ duckbill once existed have _____ some people's ideas
    46                                 47

about _____ . Many who watch movies _____ dinosaurs now
        48                             49

realize that _____ does not support what they see. These movies are
        50

just for fun.

# Form 5C  Some Reasons for the Popularity of Jogging

READER'S NAME _____

Jogging is becoming one of the fastest growing activities in the nation.

_____ people are starting to _____ each year. This, how-
____1____                              ____2____

ever, _____ a recent occurrence. It _____ not long ago that
          ____3____                            ____4____

_____ were a rare sight. _____ people thought that they
   ____5____                         ____6____

_____ quite strange. As more _____ began jogging the
   ____7____                             ____8____

sight _____ them became more common.
        ____9____

_____ are many reasons for _____ person to take up
   ____10____                          ____11____

_____ . First, it is a _____ form of exercise. This _____
   ____12____                    ____13____                            ____14____

because it involves the _____ of many parts of _____ body.
                          ____15____                      ____16____

The exercising of _____ heart is of great _____ . This is one
                    ____17____                      ____18____

of _____ most important parts of _____ human body. If the
    ____19____                             ____20____

_____ does not get the _____ exercise, serious problems can
   ____21____                     ____22____

_____ .
   ____23____

Another reason for jogging _____ for enjoyment. Besides being
                             ____24____

_____ for people, it can _____ be very much fun.
   ____25____                      ____26____

_____ of the fun of _____ comes from the opportunity
   ____27____                  ____28____

_____ provides for meeting other _____ who enjoy it.
   ____29____                              ____30____

One _____ that should be considered _____ a person
      ____31____                               ____32____

takes up _____ as a form of _____ or enjoyment is that
           ____33____                 ____34____

_____ is not for everyone. _____ should first check with
 35                                              36
_____ doctors and be prepared _____ find another form of
 37                                                      38
_____ if jogging is not _____ .
 39                                     40
Another thing is important. _____ who do not enjoy
                                              41
_____ , should not keep doing _____ . They could not expect
 42                                                43
_____ get the most out _____ jogging if they do
 44                                          45
_____ put their best effort _____ it. People who do
 46                                                47
_____ enjoy jogging would be _____ off, both mentally and
 48                                                49
_____ , if they took up another form of exercise. Those who truly enjoy
 50
jogging, however, find it a wonderful way to keep in shape.

# Form 6A  Roller Skating's Popularity over the Years

READER'S NAME _____

Roller skating has always been a favorite pastime for many children. Roller skates became

_____ standard Christmas gift. In _____ 1940s and early 1950s,
          1                                             2

_____ could be seen skating _____ most neighborhoods on their
          3                                          4

_____ steel ball bearing skates.
          5

_____ usually wore a skate _____ on a chain around
          6                                           7

_____ necks. This skate key _____ used to operate the
          8                                           9

_____ which held the skate _____ the sides of the _____
          10                                        11                              12

near the toes. A _____ buckled across the instep _____ hold the heel in
                        13                                             14

_____ .
          15

Roller skating rinks opened _____ a place for families _____
                                          16                                          17

skate indoors in safety. _____ of these rinks were _____ erected on
                                   18                                    19

large lots.

_____ the years passed, interest _____ roller skating appeared to
          20                                              21

_____ . Manufacturers gave roller skates _____ new look. A high
          22                                                        23

_____ shoe was made on _____ four wheels. The old,
          24                                   25

_____ skate key was no _____ needed.
          26                                   27

Since 1970, roller _____ has once more become _____ favorite
                              28                                         29

pastime. Children as _____ as adults are putting _____ the newest
                              30                                        31

roller skates _____ include a high top _____ , four plastic wheels, and
                        32                                      33

_____ rubber braking device attached _____ the toe of the
          34                                                35

_____ .
          36

Roller skates are not _____ providing pleasure but have _____ a
                               37                                               38

means of transportation. _____ use them to travel _____ work. Roller
                                   39                                     40

skating is _____ a good health activity, _____ it exercises the legs.
               41                                          42
_____ skating is becoming a _____ sport. Racing, roller hockey,
       43                                    44
_____ disco dancing are a _____ roller skating activities. Some
   45                                    46
_____ skaters would like roller _____ included in the olympic
   47                                    48
_____ .
   49
Rinks can now be _____ in sturdy buildings. They provide a place to learn, to
                         50
demonstrate one's skills, or just to enjoy an evening of fun.

# Form 6B  Tala and the Tribe of the Tiger

READER'S NAME _____

Long long ago, before people knew how to speak words, there lived a tribe of cave people who

worshipped tigers.

The _____ 1 of this tiger tribe _____ 2 their own weapons and

_____ 3 very bravely. Women were _____ 4 allowed to touch weapons,

_____ 5 to hunt, and if _____ 6 woman ever touched a _____ 7 ,

or hunted, she was _____ 8 to death!

In this _____ 9 tribe lived an intelligent _____ 10 girl named Tala.

Tala _____ 11 taller and swifter than _____ 12 of the girls her

_____ 13 , and she could even _____ 14 . Tala secretly wanted to

_____ 15 to make weapons, and _____ 16 hunt, for she was

_____ 17 , brave, and intelligent. So _____ 18 secretly began to make

_____ 19 and practice hunting in _____ 20 well hidden spot. Tala

_____ 21 quite expert at hunting, _____ 22 of course no one

_____ 23 her tribe knew.

One _____ 24 the tribe traveled to _____ 25 nearby river to catch

_____ 26 , and as the people _____ 27 their nets, the children

_____ 28 near the water's edge. _____ 29 , a young child ran

_____ 30 some bushes and a _____ 31 tiger grabbed the child

_____ 32 his teeth. The people _____ 33 to scream but brave

_____ 34 grabbed a spear and _____ 35 the tiger without thinking

_____ 36 the consequences.

The entire _____ 37 was grateful to Tala _____ 38 saving the child's

life, _____ 39 they quickly held a _____ 40 to decide Tala's fate.

_____ people argued and talked _____ many hours, and they
      41             42

_____ reached a decision. The _____ voted to banish brave
      43             44

_____ for thirty days and _____ nights. Tala had to _____
      45             46         47

all alone without weapons, _____ , or food. If Tala _____ , she would be
             48         49

allowed _____ live with the tribe.
        50

What do you think happened?

Cloze Passages

# Form 6C  Chopsticks

READER'S NAME _____

People in different countries use different utensils for eating. While the majority of

_____ use the conventional fork _____ knife, Chinese people use
      1                               2

_____ quite different. They use _____ with which many of
      3                               4

_____ are not familiar. They _____ two sticks known as
      5                               6

_____ .
      7

The chopsticks were first _____ of as a simpler, _____ refined way
                       8                             9

of eating. _____ food used in Chinese _____ is cut up in
              10                         11

_____ bite size pieces. This _____ of preparing food lends
      12                             13

_____ to using chopsticks. The _____ allow a person to
      14                             15

_____ with only one hand, _____ the other one free _____
      16                       17                    18

holding the bowl.

Chopsticks _____ made from many different _____ of materials.
              19                             20

Most of _____ people in southern China _____ chopsticks made from
          21                            22

bamboo _____ wood. Many wealthier people _____ families in China
          23                           24

use _____ made of more precious _____ , such as ivory or
      25                             26

_____ . These more elaborate kinds _____ chopsticks often may be
      27                           28

_____ down from one generation _____ the next.
      29                           30

The Chinese _____ their eating utensils to _____ others at the
                31                         32

table _____ when they would like _____ be excused. When someone
      33                           34

_____ to leave the table, _____ lays the chopsticks across
      35                       36

_____ bowl. The host then _____ the chopsticks, and places
      37                         38

_____ on the table. This _____ that the guest is _____
      39                     40                    41

to leave.

Copyright © 1986 by Allyn and Bacon, Inc. Use of this material is restricted to duplication from this master.

Cloze Passages      51

There are _____ 42 left-handed users of chopsticks. _____ 43 who use their left _____ 44 are corrected or punished _____ 45 their elders. The Chinese _____ 46 consider it impolite for _____ 47 to use your left _____ 48 for eating because you _____ 49 bump into the person _____ 50 the left of you.

For an exciting and different approach to eating, try using chopsticks the next time you have Chinese food.

# Form 7A  A Tall Tale about "Foolish John"

READER'S NAME _____

When I was a young girl living in the house built on stilts over the Louisiana swamp, my

grandmother once told me the story of her cousin, John LaBete. Poor John _____

1

very well-intentioned but not _____ smart. The younger cousins, _____

2                                                                                3

the English-speaking ones from _____ , teased him and called _____

4                                                                                5

Foolish John.

One day, _____ mother asked him to _____ milk the cow, but

6                                                7

_____ did not understand his _____ order and shot the

8                                                9

_____ instead. When she asked _____ he had done, John's

10                                                11

_____ mother thought for a _____ . Then, accustomed to his

12                                                13

_____ , told John to skin _____ cow and take the _____ to

14                                    15                                            16

town to sell. _____ did as his mother _____ , leaving the horns and

17                                    18

_____ hair on the hide. _____ the hide on his _____ he

19                                    20                                            21

set out for _____ . But on the way _____ heard the bayou pirates

22                                            23

_____ along the trail and, _____ frightened, he climbed a

24                                                25

_____ cypress tree and hid _____ the Spanish moss. To

26                                                27

_____ John's horror, the pirates _____ to stop under that

28                                                29

_____ tree to bury their _____ money.

30                                    31

John trembled while _____ pirates dug, muttering to _____ that

32                                                33

demons were beneath _____ . The pirates heard, looked _____ , and

34                                                    35

demanded to know _____ was there. John continued _____ about

36                                                37

demons. Suddenly one _____ the pirates screamed that _____ devil

38                                                39

himself was in _____ tree. John became so _____ that he lost his

40                                    41

_____ on the branch and _____ down into the midst
42 43

_____ the pirates—hide, hair, _____ , Spanish moss, and all.
44 45

_____ pirates were naturally so _____ by this monster which
46 47

_____ descended upon them that _____ ran off into the
48 49

_____ . Foolish John wrapped the pirates' gold in the cow's hide and carried it home
50

to his mother.

# Form 7B  The Olympics

READER'S NAME _____

Every four years, athletes from all over the world compete in the Olympics. _____ 1

country sends teams of _____ 2 finest athletes to participate _____ 3 the

games. At every _____ 4 game, old records for _____ 5 and distance are

broken _____ 6 throngs of spectators watch _____ 7 amazement.

The Olympics take _____ 8 in a different country _____ 9 time they

are held. _____ 10 before the start of _____ 11 new Olympics, the host

_____ 12 starts getting ready for _____ 13 games. A great deal

_____ 14 planning and money goes _____ 15 building an Olympic Village,

_____ 16 city with buildings to _____ 17 the teams. Stadiums, tracks,

_____ 18 gyms, rinks, and rings _____ 19 all carefully designed.

The _____ 20 open with a bright _____ 21 that is rarely seen

_____ 22 days. First the leader _____ 23 the host country is

_____ 24 into the stadium by _____ 25 head of the Olympic

_____ 26 . Then a fantastic march _____ 27 . As the bands play,

_____ 28 teams enter the stadium. _____ 29 team wears official Olympic

_____ 30 and marches behind its _____ 31 . The Greek team leads

_____ 32 march in honor of _____ 33 first Olympic games which

_____ 34 held by the Greeks. _____ 35 team of the host _____ 36

marches last.

Hundreds of _____ 37 are released all at _____ 38 , symbolizing

peaceful relations among _____ 39 . Music fills the air, _____ 40 officials

raise the Olympic _____ 41 . The interlocking rings of _____ 42 flag stand for

186002

the _____ 43 _____ of all countries and _____ 44 _____ least one of the _____ 45 _____ in the Olympic flag _____ 46 _____ on the flag of _____ 47 _____ competing country. A runner _____ 48 _____ the Olympic torch races _____ 49 _____ the track and lights _____ 50 _____ Olympic flame. During the next few weeks of competition the top athletes of the world will be determined.

Cloze Passages

# Form 7C  A Story of Two Speed Skaters

READER'S NAME _____

Almost every day, Stanley, a Polish speed skater, practiced with the other members of his team at

the ice rink in his home town of Zakopane. The year _____ 1969 and Stanley's team
                                                              1

_____ in the midst of _____ exciting season of international
        2                                3

_____ .
        4

    One day, as Stanley _____ onto the ice, he _____ that he was
                                            5                              6

being _____ by a boy of _____ thirteen. The boy, whose
              7                              8

_____ was Jan, was awkward _____ skates, but very eager
        9                                        10

_____ learn. Jan watched every _____ which Stanley made on
        11                                          12

_____ ice and tried to _____ the young man as _____ as
        13                            14                                  15

possible.

    At first, _____ was amused. Jan's career _____ a speed skater was
                        16                                  17

_____ off to a slow _____ . But Jan did not _____ trying.
        18                          19                                20

He could be _____ on the ice practicing _____ afternoon. Stanley
                    21                                      22

admired Jan's _____ and before long found _____ teaching Jan how to
                  23                                        24

_____ his form and increase _____ speed. Over the next
        25                                      26

_____ years, much progress was _____ . By the age of
        27                                        28

_____ , thanks to the help _____ Stanley, Jan had become
        29                                    30

_____ very good skater.
        31

    Soon _____ , Stanley's assistance to Jan _____ to come to an
                  32                                        33

_____ . This was because Stanley _____ moving from Zakopane,
        34                                          35

Poland _____ London, England. Before leaving, _____ , Stanley  gave
            36                                              37

Jan final _____ of encouragement. For Stanley, _____ only his
                38                                            39

relationship with _____ was ending, his career _____ a professional
                          40                                                  41
speed skater _____ ending also. Still, as _____ moved into a new
                      42                                      43
_____ , Stanley kept in touch _____ the sport through newspapers.
         44                                        45
_____ 1974, Stanley read an _____ of the world championship
         46                                        47
_____ skating competition held in _____ Italian Alps. An eighteen-
         48                                        49
_____ -old boy had easily won first place. Stanley smiled as he read the name of the
         50
winner and realized that it was his friend Jan.

# Form 8A  A Short Drive into Trouble

READER'S NAME _____

Emily was very anxious to learn how to drive, for in just one more year, she could apply for her

learner's permit to drive around town. Although one of her _____ would have to be
                                                                  1

_____ the car with her, _____ instructions, she knew it
        2                                    3

_____ be long before she _____ drive anywhere by herself.
        4                                    5

_____ now, however, Emily had _____ be contented with the
        6                                        7

_____ times her mother allowed _____ behind the wheel of
        8                                        9

_____ car. While she could _____ drive in the streets
        10                                  11

_____ , her mother occasionally permitted _____ to practice starting
        12                                                  13

the _____ in the driveway. And _____ few times, her father
         14                                      15

_____ actually let her drive _____ the parking lot at _____
        16                                      17                                  18

supermarket, after the store _____ closed and the lot _____ vacant.
                                    19                                  20

Emily was beginning _____ feel very confident in _____ driver's
                            21                                      22

seat of the _____ car. Her mother promised _____ she would teach her
                 23                                          24

_____ to back out of _____ driveway and into the _____
        25                            26                                      27

soon. Emily was certain _____ she would learn rapidly, _____ she was
                                28                                      29

sure that _____ parents would be very _____ .
                 30                                  31

One day it occurred _____ Emily that she could _____ make her
                            32                                      33

parents proud _____ demonstrating that she could _____ to back the
                     34                                          35

car _____ by herself, so she _____ to practice while they
        36                                  37

_____ shopping and surprise them _____ they got home.
        38                                          39

Emily _____ pleased when the car _____ easily the first time
            40                                  41

_____ turned the key. Taking _____ deep breath, she carefully
        42                                      43

_____ the car into reverse, _____ slowly began to back
       44                                         45

_____ of the driveway.
       46

    Suddenly _____ heard a terrible crash, _____ felt something grate
                      47                                48

under _____ car. To her horror, _____ remembered the two garbage
             49                         50

cans sitting behind the car, and then saw that they were wedged firmly beneath the dented

bumper of the car. What would her parents say now?

        Cloze Passages

# Form 8B  Gerbils

READER'S NAME _____

One of the most fascinating and easy to care for pets is the gerbil. It is gentle and

_____ very little attention.
　　　1

　　　Gerbils _____ been nicknamed pocket kangaroos _____ they
　　　　　　　　　　　2　　　　　　　　　　　　　　　　　　　　　　　　3

have strong hind _____ , can leap long distances _____ can sit up on
　　　　　　　　　4　　　　　　　　　　　　　　　　　　5

_____ haunches like a kangaroo, _____ they're small enough to
　　　6　　　　　　　　　　　　　　　　　　7

_____ in your pocket. Their _____ are furry and grow
　　　8　　　　　　　　　　　　　　　9

_____ be about four inches _____ length with a tail _____
　　　10　　　　　　　　　　　　　11　　　　　　　　　　　　　　　　12

about the same length.

_____ gerbil's day is spent _____ periods of intense activity
　　　　　13　　　　　　　　　　　　　　14

_____ by short naps. He _____ at food continually to
　　　15　　　　　　　　　　　　　　16

_____ his bursts of energy. _____ darts to and fro _____
　　　17　　　　　　　　　　　　　　18　　　　　　　　　　　　　　　19

his cage looking and _____ very much like a _____ .
　　　　　　　　　　　20　　　　　　　　　　　　　21

　　　The gerbil is a _____ curious animal always ready _____
　　　　　　　　　　　22　　　　　　　　　　　　　　　　　　23

investigate any new object _____ is placed in his _____ . If you put your
　　　　　　　　　　　　24　　　　　　　　　　　　　25

_____ in his cage, he _____ first sniff it, then _____ on it.
　　　26　　　　　　　　　　　27　　　　　　　　　　　　　28

Sudden movements _____ noises will startle him. _____ pick him up
　　　　　　　　　　29　　　　　　　　　　　　　　　30

you _____ put your hand carefully _____ him and scoop him
　　　31　　　　　　　　　　　　　　　32

_____ .
　　43

　　　Since gerbils gnaw, they _____ be housed in a _____ cage or
　　　　　　　　　　　　　　　34　　　　　　　　　　　　35

aquarium fitted _____ a water bottle and _____ least two inches of
　　　　　　　　36　　　　　　　　　　　　　37

_____ or cedar shavings. This _____ them a place to _____
　　　38　　　　　　　　　　　　　39　　　　　　　　　　　　　40

and nest. They should _____ kept in a lighted _____ , but not in direct
　　　　　　　　　　41　　　　　　　　　　　　42

_____ .
　　43

Gerbils are very clean _____ 44 _____ and bathe themselves like _____ 45 _____ .
They drink very little _____ 46 _____ do not overeat. They _____ 47 _____ eat any
commercially prepared _____ 48 _____ food as well as _____ 49 _____ vegetables.
Sunflower seeds _____ 50 _____ the gerbil's favorite treat. Gerbils are inquisitive, clean and
tame, and make great pets for children.

# Form 8C  The Race

Alfredo tightened his grip on the handlebars of his dirt bike and glanced quickly over his shoulder

at the crowds of people clustered around the sprawling course. This was Alfredo's first

_____ 1 , and his father had _____ 2 to come and watch

_____ 3 . But as all the _____ 4 moved their bikes to _____ 5

starting line, Alfredo realized _____ 6 his father would not _____ 7 to the

track in _____ 8 .

　　The starter's gun sounded _____ 9 all of the bikes _____ 10 forward.

Alfredo forgot about _____ 11 father and concentrated on _____ 12 muddy

course as he _____ 13 one turn after another. _____ 14 Alfredo had pulled

ahead _____ 15 most of the other _____ 16 , and he only had

_____ 17 pass two more to _____ 18 the lead. Dirt began _____ 19

splatter onto Alfredo's goggles _____ 20 he narrowed the distance _____ 21

his bike and the _____ 22 directly in front of _____ 23 , but Alfredo sped on,

_____ 24 to allow the others _____ 25 remain ahead of him.

_____ 26 , there was only one _____ 27 bike to pass.

　　Alfredo's _____ 28 seemed to fly over _____ 29 hills and around the

_____ 30 as he attempted to _____ 31 the leading rider. He

_____ 32 ahead and realized that _____ 33 chance for victory could

_____ 34 on the next curve.

_____ 35 began to maneuver his _____ 36 for the sharp turn

_____ 37 suddenly, above the roar _____ 38 the bikes, he heard

_____ 39 calling his name. He _____ 40 his head around and

_____ his father cheering him_____ . But at that instant,
41                                                   42

_____ felt his bike begin_____ skid. Before he knew
43                                        44

_____ , Alfredo lay sprawled beside_____ track.
45                                     46

As he scrambled_____ his feet, Alfredo knew_____ had lost the
               47                               48

race._____ when he saw his_____ running toward him with a broad
     49                                  50

smile, Alfredo felt nothing but happiness. All that mattered was that his father had come.

# Form 9A  A Beautiful and Interesting Place to Visit—Zermatt

READER'S NAME _____

Can you imagine a town which does not permit automobiles on its streets? One such

_____ , Zermatt, is nestled in _____ beautiful valley located high
     1                                  2

_____ the Swiss Alps. To _____ Zermatt, visitors could drive
     3                                  4

_____ Tasch and hike the _____ three miles up, or _____
     5                               6                               7

could ride the special _____ railroad which winds through _____
                      8                                    9

valley. Either way, the _____ little town is certainly _____ worth the
                        10                                 11

trip. During _____ winter season, Zermatt, with _____ cozy chalets,
              12                                 13

snowy peaks, _____ majestic fir trees, could _____ the perfect setting
              14                                15

for _____ Christmas card. Lucky visitors _____ even see a flock
       16                                 17

_____ mountain goats with tinkling _____ around their necks prance
     18                                  19

_____ down Main Street on _____ way to pasture. Zermatt,
     20                                  21

_____ is primarily a ski _____ , attracts visitors from all
     22                                 23

_____ the world. They come _____ enjoy the skiing, hiking,
     24                                 25

_____ entertainment and the sheer _____ of the surroundings.
     26                                 27

The _____ and most unforgettable sight, _____ , is the
               28                               29

Matterhorn. Its _____ jagged peak has lured _____ an adventurous
               30                                31

mountain climber. _____ the weather permits, the _____ can be seen
                32                               33

from _____ streets of Zermatt, and _____ are ways of getting
      34                                 35

_____ even closer look. A _____ view of the famous _____
     36                             37                        38

can be obtained by _____ the cogwheel train up _____ Gonergrat or the
                    39                               40

ski _____ to Schwarzee. These are _____ two of the areas
        41                                 42

_____ Zermatt which offer various _____ of skiing throughout the
     43                                 44

_____ . Some people might prefer _____ choose one of the
        45                                               46

_____ trails and simply hike _____ the miles of Alpine
      47                                          48

_____ .
      49

   At the end of _____ day, Main Street becomes crowded with people once more
                        50

and the rest of the evening is filled with hearty food, robust wine, and dancing and music. It is

difficult to imagine a more pleasant spot on earth to visit.

# Form 9B  The Spring Dance

READER'S NAME _____

Steve, a young man of fifteen, attended a school for boys and spent the majority of his time

studying, playing football, and running a paper route. Jenny _____ a school for girls

<br>1

_____ few miles from Steve's _____ and lived in the _____

<br>2                                          3                                 4

where he delivered newspapers _____ the afternoon.

<br>5

    Steve would _____ Jenny walking her dog _____ studying with a

<br>6                                                  7

few _____ on the front porch. _____ always smiled and greeted

<br>8                                             9

_____ when he delivered the _____ . Steve usually responded with

<br>10                                             11

_____ brief nod and solemn _____ on his face because

<br>12                                             13

_____ just couldn't avoid being _____ when he was near

<br>14                                             15

_____ .

<br>16

    More than anything in _____ world, Steve wanted to _____ her to

<br>17                                             18

his school's _____ Dance, but he imagined _____ she had plenty of

<br>19                                             20

_____ and wouldn't be interested _____ going with him anyway.

<br>21                                             22

_____ his friends inquired about _____ plans for the dance,

<br>23                                             24

_____ pretended to be indifferent, _____ they urged him to

<br>25                                             26

_____ going to the dance. _____ finally decided that he

<br>27                                           28

_____ make the effort to _____ Jenny, but felt sure _____

<br>29                                          30                                     31

he would be turned _____ .

<br>32

    On the following afternoon, _____ Steve was delivering papers,

<br>33

_____ could see Jenny sitting _____ the front steps. She

<br>34                                             35

_____ to be waiting for _____ . Steve grew more nervous

<br>36                                             37

_____ he approached her, pretending _____ be busy with his

<br>38                                          39

_____ . By the time he _____ managed to say hello, _____
    40                             41                          42

courage had failed, and _____ had given up the _____ of asking her to
                             43                           44

_____ dance.
    45

    To his surprise, _____ suddenly struck up a _____ , and a few
                            46                         47

minutes _____ had asked him to _____ Spring Dance being held
                   48                       49

_____ her school. The turn of events was so startling to Steve that, for a few
    50

moments, he could only stare in total amazement.

# Form 9C  Penguins

READER'S NAME _____

A penguin is an unusual bird that stands upright on short legs and walks with an amusing,

clumsy waddle. Penguins live _____ the southern half of _____ world.
                                      **1**                                      **2**
Several kinds live _____ the frozen ice of _____ Antarctic. Others are
                            **3**                              **4**
located _____ north in areas touched _____ cold ocean currents that
               **5**                                    **6**
_____ in Antarctica. Penguins are _____ attractions in zoos but
        **7**                                        **8**
_____ difficult to keep in _____ because they catch diseases
        **9**                              **10**
_____ .
     **11**

Penguins lost the ability _____ fly millions of years _____ when
                                  **12**                                  **13**
their wings developed _____ flippers which serve as _____ in the
                              **14**                                    **15**
water. These _____ , along with webbed feet, _____ penguins fantastic
                    **16**                                      **17**
swimmers and _____ . Their short, dense feathers _____ a waterproof
                    **18**                                          **19**
coat, and _____ layers of fat keep _____ insulated from cold weather.
                 **20**                              **21**
_____ eat fish, and spend _____ of their lives in
        **22**                              **23**
_____ waters, but lay eggs _____ raise their young on
        **24**                                **25**
_____ . While on land they _____ their nests in enormous
        **26**                                **27**
_____ called rookeries. A single _____ may contain as many
        **28**                                    **29**
_____ a million penguins. Most _____ make their nests on
        **30**                                  **31**
_____ ground, and lay their _____ in shallow hollows scraped
        **32**                                **33**
_____ the icy dirt. Some _____ the species lay eggs _____
        **34**                          **35**                                      **36**
tunnels dug in the _____ .
                          **37**

The largest member of _____ penguin family, the emperor _____ ,
                              **38**                                      **39**
breeds on the sea _____ in the bitter cold _____ darkness of the
                          **40**                              **41**
Antarctic _____ . This is the only _____ of the species in
                 **42**                              **43**

_____ the male does all _____ incubating. He goes without
      44                            45

_____ for two months while _____ holds the single egg
      46                            47

_____ top of his feet _____ keep it off the _____ . When
      48                       49                         50

the chick hatches, the female returns from the sea to feed it, and the male goes off to feed on

shrimp, the staple food of penguins in Antarctica.

                Cloze Passages

# Form 10A  The Amazing Pyramids

READER'S NAME _____

The Superdome and World Trade Center are both great feats of modern engineering. However,

human beings have _____ building amazing structures for _____ of
              1                                2

years, and when _____ stop to think about _____ limited technology
               3                      4

used to _____ some of these early _____ , you may think they
          5                6

_____ even more amazing than _____ ones.
       7                8

    The Egyptian pyramids _____ examples of structures built _____
                   9                      10

limited technology. Though the _____ Egyptians had only simple _____
                       11                  12

made of wood, stone, _____ and brass, they were _____ to cut, move,
               13                  14

and _____ stones that weighed many _____ each in order to
       15                16

_____ their pyramids. These were _____ well-constructed that they
       17                18

_____ stand today.
       19

    The pyramids _____ huge. They sit on _____ square bases and
               20              21

have _____ smooth, triangular sides that _____ to a sharp point
       22               23

_____ the top. All were _____ by slaves, who worked
       24           25

_____ the direction of Egyptian _____ . Many lives were lost
       26           27

_____ many people were badly _____ during the hundreds of
       28           29

_____ the pyramids were under _____ .
       30           31

    The pyramids were built _____ house the dead bodies _____
                   32                  33

Egyptian kings. The Egyptians _____ that a person's soul _____ live
                     34              35

forever, as long _____ the body was cared _____ . Therefore, when an
          36             37

Egyptian _____ died, his body was _____ inside a pyramid, along
       38           39

_____ most of his valuable _____ , a lot of food _____
       40           41           42

Copyright © 1986 by Allyn and Bacon, Inc. Use of this material is restricted to duplication from this master.

Cloze Passages      71

drink, and sometimes even _____ wife, family, and servants. _____
43                                                      44
pyramid was then sealed _____ keep the king safe.
45
_____ later times, many of _____ pyramids were broken into
46                                        47
_____ looted by robbers. But _____ pyramids stand today as
48                                        49
_____ monuments to the civilization that created them. They are just one example of
50
amazing structures created by ancient man.

# Form 10B  Life in a Rock Band

READER'S NAME  _____

Michael slowly placed his guitar in its case and propped it upright against an amplifier. He

surveyed the now _____ illuminated gymnasium and watched _____
1        2

the remaining couples walked _____ the discarded paper cups _____
3        4

fallen prom decorations littering _____ dance floor, leaving him _____
5        6

the other band members _____ to pack their equipment _____ the van.
7        8

Somehow, this _____ not quite how he _____ imagined life in a
9        10

_____ band would be.
11

Michael _____ the afternoon, two years _____ , that he and his
12        13

_____ had agreed to form _____ group. They had assumed
14        15

_____ the band would be _____ great demand in nightspots
16        17

_____ the city within a _____ . And they had all _____
18        19        20

that one of their _____ big expenditures would be _____ hiring of a
21        22

stage _____ to set up their _____ before each performance and
23        24

_____ it all up afterwards.
25

_____ had relished the anticipated _____ of their friends. They
26        27

_____ imagined the adulation that _____ fans would bestow upon
28        29

_____ once they began their _____ concert tour. After some
30        31

_____ discussion, they had conceded _____ a concert tour was
32        33

_____ unlikely, at least until _____ made some records. But
34        35

_____ of them was sure _____ a recording contract would
36        37

_____ easy to get once _____ talent was recognized.
38        39

Well, _____ the band was in _____ demand. Any school group
40        41

_____ could not afford to _____ a well-known band _____
42        43        44

them to play for _____ dances. They barely earned _____ money to pay
                              45                                          46

for _____ van and the gas _____ consumed. The thought of
                47                                48

_____ stage crew was ludicrous.
            49

_____ he made a final trip out to the van parked in the empty schoolyard,
            50

Michael laughed ruefully as he recalled their dreams of cheering fans and recording contracts. He

knew the time had come to leave the band.

                Cloze Passages

# Form 10C  The Great Houdini

READER'S NAME _____

Simply reading or hearing the name, Houdini, brings to mind thoughts of magic and great

escapes. Years ago, Harry Houdini _____ famous for performances in
                                         1

_____ he released himself from _____ and handcuffs. His challenging
        2                                         3

_____ included freeing himself from _____ , straight jackets, and
        4                                              5

various _____ cells around the world.
              6

_____ stage career began very _____ when, as a young
        7                                         8

_____ he performed acrobatic feats _____ a circus, calling himself
        9                                              10

_____ . Later he took the _____ Houdini in honor of _____
        11                              12                                         13

famous magician for whom _____ had great admiration.
                                14

Soon _____ this, he began working _____ dime museums and
            15                                         16

vaudeville _____ , traveling all over the _____ . During one of these
                17                                         18

_____ , he attracted the attention _____ an influential producer who
        19                                         20

_____ him to specialize in _____ . His fame spread as
        21                              22

_____ perfected these and his _____ acts.
        23                                 24

In response to _____ challenge, he once allowed _____ to be
                      25                                         26

locked in _____ trunk. This was then _____ in steel tape, and
              27                                         28

_____ into a river. Thousands _____ spectators waited breathlessly for
        29                                     30

_____ a full minute until _____ Great Houdini finally reappeared,
        31                                 32

_____ of his shackles.
        33

As _____ as Houdini's spectacular feats _____ to those who
          34                                                 35

viewed _____ , he refused to describe _____ as supernatural. Claims by
            36                                         37

_____ that he had such _____ made him angry enough
        38                              39

_____ publish an investigation of _____ practices. Houdini prided
        40                                         41

himself _____ the fact that his _____ could be logically explained
             42                                  43

_____ understood by anyone of _____ intelligence.
       44                                  45

    Harry Houdini died _____ Halloween night, after telling _____
                             46                                   47

wife that he would _____ his greatest feat, an _____ from death, and
                        48                               49

return _____ her on an anniversary of his demise. Unfortunately, he never managed
             50

to perfect that act.

Cloze Passages

# Form 11A  A Misadventure into a Foreign Country

READER'S NAME _____

Ellen and Myra were very excited to reach Dubrovnik, Yugoslavia after an overnight ferry ride.

_____ 1 _____ had long been intrigued _____ 2 _____ the prospect of visiting _____ 3 _____ communist country. They soon _____ 4 _____, however, that they were _____ 5 _____ well prepared to enter _____ 6 _____ a different world.

The _____ 7 _____ of Dubrovnik did possess _____ 8 _____ genuine old world charm, _____ 9 _____ they found its people _____ 10 _____ be unfriendly to strangers _____ 11 _____ unwilling to attempt communication. _____ 12 _____ girls, therefore, decided to _____ 13 _____ their stay in the _____ 14 _____ and drive leisurely through _____ 15 _____ countryside which lay between _____ 16 _____ and their final destination _____ 17 _____ Athens, Greece. They envisioned _____ 18 _____ villages and friendly peasants _____ 19 _____ fruits and cheeses on _____ 20 _____ roadside, but instead they _____ 21 _____ seemingly endless miles of _____ 22 _____ road, with only two _____ 23 _____ villages situated along the _____ 24 _____ stretch.

As hunger set _____ 25 _____ they stopped at an _____ 26 _____ café but found the _____ 27 _____ grossly unappealing. They next _____ 28 _____ for a grocery or _____ 29 _____ in order to purchase _____ 30 _____ makings for a picnic. _____ 31 _____ grocery was stocked primarily _____ 32 _____ dusty canned goods that _____ 33 _____ not labeled.

Many hours _____ 34 _____ they crossed the border _____ 35 _____ Yugoslavia and Greece. Soon _____ 36 _____ they were relating their _____ 37 _____ of woe to English _____ 38 _____ whom they met. The _____ 39 _____ were surprised to hear _____ 40 _____ these people had enjoyed _____ 41 _____. Apparently, friendly people and _____ 42 _____ sights could be found _____ 43 _____. These more experienced travelers

_____ that the two girls _____ both been affected by
44                                45
_____ phenomenon called culture shock, _____ by a lack of
46                                                47
_____ for a visit to _____ very different culture. The
48                          49
_____ girls admitted that this could be true. They decided to reserve their judgment
50
until after a second visit.

# Form 11B How Students Find Jobs

READER'S NAME _____

The subject of employment is of prime concern to nearly every high school senior. Most students

would _____ a part time job _____ school hours, on weekends
          1                                    2

_____ during vacations. Those who _____ to attend college often
        3                                         4

_____ a part-time job _____ help cover expenses. Students
       5                              6

_____ do not intend to _____ their education have the
       7                              8

_____ task before them of _____ an interesting position with
       9                                  10

_____ promising future. Locating and _____ such employment is an
       11                                    12

_____ that takes planning, perseverance, _____ an understanding of
       13                                              14

what _____ seek in a prospective _____ .
            15                                  16

One of the most _____ methods employed by students _____ their
                      17                                          18

search for a _____ job is to read _____ classified section of the
                 19                              20

_____ . It requires time and _____ to sift through the
       21                                  22

_____ assortment of jobs in _____ want ads to find _____
       23                                 24                                    25

handful that are worth _____ . The classified ads are _____ into
                            26                                       27

sections. Wise students _____ have several types of _____ in mind but
                             28                                    29

not _____ time reading about jobs _____ which they are not
        30                                       31

_____ .
       32

Finding an interesting position _____ is only the beginning. _____
                                      33                                    34

next step is to _____ a letter requesting consideration _____ the
                     35                                               36

position. This letter _____ often accompanied by a _____ containing an
                           37                                    38

impressive yet _____ description of the student's _____ .
                    39                                          40

Those students who submit _____ good letter of application _____
                               41                                          42

a résumé are usually _____ a personal interview. The _____ can be the
                          43                                       44

deciding _____ . This is frequently the _____ at which the prospective
45                                                  46

_____ determines whether or not _____ applicant has potential to
47                                                  48

_____ an asset to the _____ . Students who project themselves as neat,
49                                  50

cooperative, responsible individuals have an excellent chance of being offered the job they seek.

# Form 11C  Teenagers and Shyness

READER'S NAME _____

People who are afraid to express their feelings or are afraid to start a conversation with a stranger
may be said to suffer from some type of shyness. Many psychologists believe _____
_1_
teenagers experience shyness more _____ any other age group. _____
_2_                                                    _3_
psychologists theorize that shyness _____ caused by the great _____ on
_4_                                                    _5_
the part of _____ teens to feel popular _____ school and by their
_6_                                        _7_
_____ to feel physically attractive. _____ who do not feel
_8_                                                    _9_
_____ or attractive may isolate _____ from others and develop
_10_                                          _11_
_____ negative self-image.
_12_

    Shyness _____ assume several forms. Among _____ is bashful-
_13_                                          _14_
ness, a form _____ shyness characteristic of children _____
_15_                                                              _16_
adolescents, in which a _____ is inclined to shrink _____ public
_17_                                          _18_
attention. Another form, _____ diffidence, is a distrust _____ one's own
_19_                                          _20_
ability or _____ that causes hesitation in _____ acting or speaking.
_21_                                          _22_
Modesty _____ a form of shyness _____ suggests an absence of
_23_                                          _24_
_____ ; and coyness is shyness _____ appears to be affected.
_25_                                          _26_
_____ shyness can be a _____ experience, it is far
_27_                                          _28_
_____ a hopeless situation. Teenagers _____ learn to overcome it
_29_                                          _30_
_____ having their self-confidence _____ by others. When teenagers
_31_                                          _32_
_____ praised for their talents _____ abilities their self-image
_33_                                          _34_
_____ improves. It is then _____ for self help to _____ .
_35_                                          _36_                                  _37_
One way to accomplish _____ is for teenagers to _____ reasonable
_38_                                          _39_
goals for themselves _____ that shyness is overcome _____ gradual
_40_                                          _41_
stages. For example, _____ teenager could plan to _____ at least one
_42_                                          _43_

new _____ each day at school. _____ usually find that once
        44                                    45
_____ barrier is broken, it _____ easier to meet new
     46                               47
_____ . In addition, as teenagers _____ and have more experiences
     48                                    49
_____ school and other social situations, they feel increasingly more relaxed with
     50
people. Teens, therefore, need not be too disturbed by a stage of shyness in their lives.

# Form 12A  A Difficult Decision

READER'S NAME _____

Steve sat in his room, gazing vacantly at the textbook propped open before him. He was supposed

to _____ studying for his final _____ , yet he could not
      1                                2

_____ his thoughts from wandering _____ to the discussion he
      3                             4

_____ had with his parents _____ dinner. Actually, the word
      5                         6

_____ would better describe the _____ that had terminated with
      7                         8

_____ abrupt exit from the _____ .
      9                       10

    Despite his parents' strenuous _____ , Steve was convinced that
                      11

_____ was correct in deciding _____ forgo college for a
      12                         13

_____ so that he could _____ through Europe with his
      14                       15

_____ friend's family. He firmly _____ that the educational
      16                       17

experiences _____ would have in Europe _____ far outweigh the
           18                   19

benefits _____ attending freshman classes at _____ university for a
         20                   21

few _____ credit. Steve was also _____ about the damage that
       22                   23

_____ be done to his _____ with his girl friend _____ he
      24               25               26

shunned her parent's _____ offer, although he did _____ mention this
              27                   28

to his _____ .
      29

    Yet it seemed that _____ parents were aware of _____ concern,
                      30                 31

because they had _____ on the idea that _____ separation from his girl
              32               33

_____ might be beneficial. They _____ that a good relationship
      34                   35

_____ withstand any problems caused _____ the separation. Their
      36                   37

biggest _____ , however, was that Steve _____ fall so far behind
         38                   39

_____ current classmates that he _____ not want to go
      40                   41

_____ college at all. They _____ to feel that attending
      42                   43

_____ classes with some of_____ friends would motivate Steve
     44                             45

_____ remain in school and_____ diligently toward a degree.
     46                             47

_____ attention suddenly shifted back _____ the book in front
      48                             49

_____ him. If he didn't study for his exam, the question of whether to attend college
     50

or not would be settled for him.

        Cloze Passages

# Form 12B  Procrastination

READER'S NAME _____

Procrastination, an ailment which affects many students, is defined as putting off doing some-

thing until a future time, or postponing needlessly. This affliction _____ students of
1

all ages, _____ , and levels of education. _____ most commonly occurs
2                                                        3

when _____ such as term papers, _____ , and readings are made.
4                                              5

_____ are several reasons why _____ students wait until the
6                                            7

_____ possible moment to begin _____ assignments. One reason for
8                                              9

_____ may be that they _____ clinging to a hope _____
10                                  11                              12

the assignment will be _____ , or maybe even completely _____ .
13                                                          14

Another possible reason may _____ that the student is _____ for divine
15                                                16

intervention either _____ the actual completing of _____ assignment
17                                                18

or at least _____ providing inspiration. A common _____ of students
19                                                20

when questioned _____ why they procrastinate is _____ there is
21                                                22

something that _____ would rather be doing. _____ , they put off the
23                                              24

_____ desirable activity. Unfortunately, virtually _____ activity is
25                                                              26

more desirable _____ writing a term paper, _____ a text, or studying
27                                              28

_____ a test.
29

The student _____ has procrastinated too long _____ displays
30                                                    31

symptoms such as _____ anxiety, headaches, stomach aches, _____
32                                                              33

other physical ailments which _____ the effective completion of _____
34                                                          35

assignment. The young procrastinator _____ often try to enlist _____
36                                            37

parents' aid in meeting _____ . Unfortunately, the older one _____ ,
38                                                          39

the more responsibility one _____ to assume for meeting _____ , and
40                                                  41

the more costly _____ becomes.
42

186002

In an effort _____ 43 _____ aid students in overcoming _____ 44 _____ , teachers frequently establish intermediate _____ 45 _____ before the final work _____ 46 _____ due. Frequently, this strategy _____ 47 _____ serves the purpose of _____ 48 _____ more opportunities for students _____ 49 _____ procrastinate. There appears to _____ 50 _____ no cure for procrastination. While most procrastinators would like to change, they usually wait until some better time to do so.

# Form 12C  A New Breed of Campers

READER'S NAME _____

An amazing phenomenon happens every spring. People exchange their suburban

_____ for the opportunity to _____ with nature. They are
       1                                 2

_____ the millions of Americans _____ love to go camping,
       3                                 4

_____ they come in two _____ distinct varieties.
       5                         6

The first _____ includes the wilderness campers; _____ sincerely
            7                                8

enjoy roughing it. _____ thrive on peace and _____ , and the lack of
             9                         10

_____ the most basic amenities _____ them completely undaunted
     11                          12

because _____ genuinely enjoy getting away _____ it all. They can
          13                        14

_____ found in parks or _____ rustic settings, but wherever
     15                     16

_____ go, the area is _____ to abound with much _____
     17               18                        19
nature's teeming beauty.

However, _____ is a burgeoning group _____ little resemblance to
          20                         21

the _____ . This second group is _____ considered by the uninitiated
       22                         23

_____ include the luckiest campers _____ they possess one of
     24                         25

_____ man's most questionable inventions— _____ recreational
     26                         27

vehicle. They populate _____ of the same havens _____ by the
          28                     29

wilderness camper, _____ to the latter's displeasure. _____
          30                     31

requirements are many; beds, _____ , and air conditioners are _____
                  32                      33

equipment for this species. _____ tape players, radios, and _____
                34                     35

compete for dominance in _____ atmosphere resembling cacophony.
                36

They _____ converge on an otherwise _____ setting and proceed
       37                        38

to _____ the worst of suburban _____ . Not for them is
     39                     40

_____ beauty of a sunset _____ the orchestra of the _____ ;
     41               42                      43

they are too busy _____ 44 with the people in _____ 45 next camper who bear _____ 46 curious resemblance to their _____ 47 back home, or they _____ 48 too anxious that they _____ 49 miss the continued misdeeds _____ 50 a certain villain on television. Why they ever leave home is a question to confound the best of modern philosophers.

# Cloze Passage Coding
# Form and Answer Keys

◆◆◆◆◆◆◆◆◆◆◆◆◆◆◆◆◆◆◆◆◆◆◆

READER'S NAME ———————————————— PASSAGE NO. ————

SCORER ———————————————— DATE ————

*De Santi
Cloze Reading
Inventory*

| DN | Word deleted | Reader's choice | Coding categories | | | | | |
|---|---|---|---|---|---|---|---|---|
| | | | Blank | Exact | C&C | Sem | None | NGS |
| 1 | | | | | | | | |
| 2 | | | | | | | | |
| 3 | | | | | | | | |
| 4 | | | | | | | | |
| 5 | | | | | | | | |
| 6 | | | | | | | | |
| 7 | | | | | | | | |
| 8 | | | | | | | | |
| 9 | | | | | | | | |
| 10 | | | | | | | | |
| 11 | | | | | | | | |
| 12 | | | | | | | | |
| 13 | | | | | | | | |
| 14 | | | | | | | | |
| 15 | | | | | | | | |
| 16 | | | | | | | | |
| 17 | | | | | | | | |
| 18 | | | | | | | | |
| 19 | | | | | | | | |
| 20 | | | | | | | | |
| 21 | | | | | | | | |
| 22 | | | | | | | | |
| 23 | | | | | | | | |
| 24 | | | | | | | | |
| 25 | | | | | | | | |

| DN | Word deleted | Reader's choice | Coding categories | | | | | |
|----|--------------|-----------------|-------|-------|-----|-----|------|-----|
|    |              |                 | Blank | Exact | C&C | Sem | None | NGS |
| 26 |              |                 |       |       |     |     |      |     |
| 27 |              |                 |       |       |     |     |      |     |
| 28 |              |                 |       |       |     |     |      |     |
| 29 |              |                 |       |       |     |     |      |     |
| 30 |              |                 |       |       |     |     |      |     |
| 31 |              |                 |       |       |     |     |      |     |
| 32 |              |                 |       |       |     |     |      |     |
| 33 |              |                 |       |       |     |     |      |     |
| 34 |              |                 |       |       |     |     |      |     |
| 35 |              |                 |       |       |     |     |      |     |
| 36 |              |                 |       |       |     |     |      |     |
| 37 |              |                 |       |       |     |     |      |     |
| 38 |              |                 |       |       |     |     |      |     |
| 39 |              |                 |       |       |     |     |      |     |
| 40 |              |                 |       |       |     |     |      |     |
| 41 |              |                 |       |       |     |     |      |     |
| 42 |              |                 |       |       |     |     |      |     |
| 43 |              |                 |       |       |     |     |      |     |
| 44 |              |                 |       |       |     |     |      |     |
| 45 |              |                 |       |       |     |     |      |     |
| 46 |              |                 |       |       |     |     |      |     |
| 47 |              |                 |       |       |     |     |      |     |
| 48 |              |                 |       |       |     |     |      |     |
| 49 |              |                 |       |       |     |     |      |     |
| 50 |              |                 |       |       |     |     |      |     |

Total number

Total percent

Traditional comprehension

Total comprehension

Logical language usage

Structure of language (100% − TP NGS)

## FORM 3A

1. is
2. about
3. it
4. snowmen
5. fights
6. the
7. is
8. see
9. gets
10. a
11. can
12. is
13. caps
14. starts
15. ending
16. plants
17. new
18. just
19. sports
20. of
21. of
22. birds
23. shells
24. eating
25. follows
26. land
27. are
28. are
29. it
30. for
31. going
32. leaves
33. of
34. has
35. many
36. are
37. get
38. begin
39. many
40. south
41. bury
42. at
43. and
44. fall
45. football
46. is
47. too
48. the
49. the
50. then

## FORM 3B

1. have
2. city
3. an
4. no
5. a
6. boy
7. dreamed
8. James
9. which
10. would
11. take
12. the
13. the
14. would
15. have
16. of
17. and
18. treat
19. lumps
20. his
21. with
22. family
23. the
24. gotten
25. job
26. sad
27. to
28. attend
29. upset
30. few
31. moved
32. registered
33. which
34. from
35. to
36. school
37. made
38. was
39. friends
40. to
41. was
42. discussed
43. now
44. and
45. for
46. pony
47. get
48. birthday
49. surprise
50. his

**FORM 3C**

1. are
2. these
3. in
4. koalas
5. of
6. of
7. trees
8. down
9. of
10. name
11. koalas
12. knowing
13. feed
14. each
15. first
16. off
17. they
18. to
19. is
20. than
21. baby
22. pouch
23. there
24. that
25. or

26. mother's
27. young
28. mothers
29. year
30. strong
31. with
32. can
33. on
34. in
35. most
36. eat
37. live
38. groups
39. sharp
40. of
41. live
42. find
43. proper
44. the
45. the
46. where
47. koalas
48. this
49. koalas
50. by

**FORM 4A**

1. going
2. campout
3. entire
4. they
5. a
6. listen
7. she
8. ditch
9. keep
10. it
11. them
12. extra
13. they
14. Paul
15. had
16. he
17. would
18. from
19. of
20. to
21. the
22. it
23. of
24. of
25. sure

26. enough
27. to
28. animals
29. their
30. didn't
31. be
32. to
33. whistles
34. to
35. other
36. soon
37. found
38. and
39. they
40. some
41. flashlights
42. but
43. they
44. important
45. any
46. at
47. her
48. they
49. opened
50. tent

FORM 4B

1. of
2. doing
3. amazing
4. lion
5. with
6. a
7. when
8. and
9. if
10. attack
11. you
12. growls
13. the
14. dogs
15. tricks
16. walk
17. and
18. noses
19. teach
20. and
21. it
22. a
23. many
24. in
25. time

26. use
27. in
28. has
29. the
30. even
31. audience
32. and
33. eyes
34. hard
35. see
36. accomplished
37. holding
38. watch
39. the
40. to
41. is
42. tight
43. the
44. laugh
45. the
46. always
47. stunts
48. they
49. they
50. fall

FORM 4C

1. have
2. with
3. snakes
4. and
5. lizards
6. if
7. by
8. off
9. later
10. new
11. reptiles
12. and
13. snakes
14. have
15. sharp
16. snakes
17. with
18. small
19. alligators
20. big
21. most
22. the
23. trouble
24. an
25. called

26. has
27. and
28. has
29. another
30. turtle
31. eggs
32. out
33. lay
34. beach
35. sea
36. down
37. home
38. reptiles
39. very
40. in
41. easy
42. hard
43. match
44. are
45. are
46. you
47. reptiles
48. city's
49. beautiful
50. part

Cloze Passage Coding Form and Answer Keys

## FORM 5A

1. father
2. turn
3. the
4. his
5. of
6. this
7. trip
8. Tom
9. his
10. with
11. could
12. up
13. sunshine
14. jackets
15. puffy
16. blue
17. silence
18. broken
19. chirping
20. glided
21. back
22. forest
23. the
24. Tom
25. his
26. pitching
27. was
28. of
29. wrong
30. the
31. hear
32. of
33. pulled
34. to
35. the
36. was
37. hands
38. speed
39. them
40. hang
41. could
42. other
43. lashed
44. soon
45. Tom
46. the
47. over
48. for
49. once
50. a

## FORM 5B

1. while
2. exciting
3. a
4. scientists
5. animals
6. man
7. other
8. been
9. in
10. are
11. with
12. their
13. size
14. of
15. most
16. look
17. the
18. many
19. meat
20. plants
21. others
22. never
23. for
24. ate
25. already
26. by
27. dinosaurs
28. either
29. others
30. huge
31. dinosaurs
32. strange
33. and
34. dinosaur
35. odd
36. fat
37. waddle
38. its
39. quite
40. and
41. was
42. that
43. bill
44. its
45. that
46. the
47. changed
48. dinosaurs
49. about
50. science

**FORM 5C**

1. more
2. jog
3. is
4. was
5. joggers
6. some
7. looked
8. people
9. of
10. there
11. a
12. jogging
13. good
14. is
15. use
16. the
17. the
18. benefit
19. the
20. the
21. heart
22. needed
23. occur
24. is
25. good
26. also
27. part
28. jogging
29. it
30. people
31. thing
32. when
33. jogging
34. exercise
35. it
36. people
37. their
38. to
39. exercise
40. recommended
41. people
42. jogging
43. it
44. to
45. of
46. not
47. into
48. not
49. better
50. physically

**FORM 6A**

1. a
2. the
3. children
4. in
5. new
6. skaters
7. key
8. their
9. was
10. clamps
11. to
12. shoe
13. strap
14. to
15. place
16. providing
17. to
18. many
19. tents
20. as
21. in
22. decline
23. a
24. top
25. the
26. trusted
27. longer
28. skating
29. a
30. well
31. on
32. which
33. shoe
34. a
35. to
36. skate
37. only
38. become
39. people
40. to
41. also
42. because
43. roller
44. big
45. and
46. few
47. expert
48. skating
49. games
50. found

FORM 6B

1. men
2. made
3. fought
4. not
5. or
6. any
7. weapon
8. put
9. fierce
10. young
11. was
12. all
13. age
14. swim
15. learn
16. to
17. strong
18. she
19. weapons
20. a
21. became
22. but
23. in
24. day
25. a

26. fish
27. cast
28. played
29. suddenly
30. into
31. huge
32. between
33. began
34. Tala
35. killed
36. about
37. tribe
38. for
39. but
40. meeting
41. the
42. for
43. finally
44. tribe
45. Tala
46. thirty
47. live
48. fire
49. survived
50. to

FORM 6C

1. people
2. and
3. something
4. utensils
5. us
6. use
7. chopsticks
8. thought
9. more
10. most
11. cooking
12. small
13. way
14. itself
15. chopsticks
16. eat
17. leaving
18. for
19. are
20. types
21. the
22. use
23. or
24. and
25. chopsticks

26. materials
27. silver
28. of
29. passed
30. to
31. use
32. let
33. know
34. to
35. wants
36. he
37. his
38. removes
39. them
40. means
41. free
42. no
43. children
44. hand
45. by
46. would
47. you
48. hand
49. would
50. to

## FORM 7A

1. was
2. too
3. particularly
4. town
5. him
6. John's
7. go
8. he
9. mother's
10. cow
11. what
12. patient
13. minute
14. mistakes
15. the
16. hide
17. John
18. asked
19. the
20. carrying
21. back
22. town
23. he
24. coming
25. being
26. large
27. among
28. poor
29. decided
30. very
31. stolen
32. the
33. himself
34. him
35. up
36. who
37. muttering
38. of
39. the
40. the
41. terrified
42. hold
43. tumbled
44. of
45. horns
46. the
47. scared
48. had
49. they
50. swamp

## FORM 7B

1. each
2. its
3. in
4. olympic
5. speed
6. as
7. in
8. place
9. each
10. years
11. a
12. country
13. the
14. of
15. into
16. a
17. house
18. pools
19. are
20. olympics
21. splash
22. these
23. of
24. welcomed
25. the
26. committee
27. begins
28. the
29. each
30. dress
31. flag
32. the
33. the
34. were
35. the
36. country
37. birds
38. once
39. countries
40. and
41. banner
42. the
43. brotherhood
44. at
45. colors
46. is
47. each
48. bearing
49. around
50. the

## FORM 7C

1. was
2. was
3. an
4. competition
5. skated
6. noticed
7. followed
8. about
9. name
10. on
11. to
12. move
13. the
14. imitate
15. closely
16. Stanley
17. as
18. certainly
19. start
20. quit
21. seen
22. every
23. determination
24. himself
25. improve
26. his
27. few
28. evident
29. fifteen
30. of
31. a
32. however
33. was
34. end
35. was
36. to
37. however
38. words
39. not
40. Jan
41. as
42. was
43. he
44. life
45. with
46. in
47. account
48. speed
49. the
50. year

## FORM 8A

1. parents
2. in
3. giving
4. wouldn't
5. could
6. for
7. to
8. few
9. her
10. the
11. not
12. yet
13. her
14. car
15. a
16. had
17. in
18. the
19. was
20. was
21. to
22. the
23. family
24. that
25. how
26. the
27. street
28. that
29. and
30. her
31. proud
32. to
33. really
34. by
35. learn
36. out
37. decided
38. were
39. when
40. was
41. started
42. she
43. a
44. shifted
45. and
46. out
47. she
48. and
49. the
50. she

## FORM 8B

1. requires
2. have
3. because
4. legs
5. and
6. their
7. yet
8. fit
9. bodies
10. to
11. in
12. of
13. the
14. in
15. followed
16. nibbles
17. support
18. he
19. in
20. acting
21. chipmunk
22. highly
23. to
24. that
25. cage
26. hand
27. will
28. crawl
29. or
30. to
31. should
32. under
33. up
34. should
35. metal
36. with
37. at
38. wood
39. provides
40. burrow
41. be
42. room
43. sunlight
44. animals
45. cats
46. and
47. will
48. gerbil
49. fresh
50. are

## FORM 8C

1. competition
2. promised
3. him
4. boys
5. the
6. that
7. get
8. time
9. and
10. roared
11. his
12. the
13. rounded
14. soon
15. of
16. riders
17. to
18. take
19. to
20. as
21. between
22. one
23. him
24. refusing
25. to
26. soon
27. more
28. bike
29. the
30. curves
31. overtake
32. peered
33. his
34. come
35. Alfredo
36. bike
37. when
38. of
39. someone
40. jerked
41. spotted
42. on
43. he
44. to
45. it
46. the
47. to
48. he
49. but
50. father

**FORM 9A**

1. town
2. a
3. in
4. reach
5. to
6. final
7. they
8. mountain
9. the
10. picturesque
11. well
12. the
13. its
14. and
15. provide
16. a
17. might
18. of
19. bells
20. merrily
21. their
22. which
23. resort
24. over
25. to
26. nightly
27. beauty
28. biggest
29. however
30. dramatically
31. many
32. when
33. Matterhorn
34. the
35. there
36. an
37. magnificent
38. peak
39. taking
40. to
41. lift
42. but
43. surrounding
44. forms
45. year
46. to
47. many
48. through
49. splendor
50. the

**FORM 9B**

1. attended
2. a
3. school
4. neighborhood
5. in
6. notice
7. or
8. classmates
9. she
10. Steve
11. newspaper
12. a
13. expression
14. he
15. nervous
16. her
17. the
18. ask
19. Spring
20. that
21. dates
22. in
23. when
24. his
25. Steve
26. but
27. consider
28. Steve
29. would
30. ask
31. that
32. down
33. as
34. he
35. on
36. appeared
37. someone
38. as
39. to
40. newspaper
41. finally
42. his
43. he
44. idea
45. the
46. Jenny
47. conversation
48. later
49. the
50. at

**FORM 9C**

1. in
2. the
3. on
4. the
5. farther
6. by
7. originate
8. popular
9. are
10. captivity
11. easily
12. to
13. ago
14. into
15. paddles
16. flippers
17. make
18. divers
19. form
20. thick
21. them
22. penguins
23. much
24. antarctic
25. and
26. land
27. make
28. colonies
29. rookery
30. as
31. species
32. bare
33. eggs
34. in
35. of
36. in
37. ground
38. the
39. penguin
40. ice
41. and
42. winter
43. member
44. which
45. the
46. food
47. he
48. on
49. to
50. ice

**FORM 10A**

1. been
2. hundreds
3. you
4. the
5. build
6. structures
7. are
8. modern
9. are
10. with
11. ancient
12. tools
13. copper
14. able
15. raise
16. tons
17. build
18. so
19. still
20. are
21. perfect
22. four
23. rise
24. at
25. built
26. under
27. overseers
28. and
29. injured
30. years
31. construction
32. to
33. of
34. believed
35. could
36. as
37. for
38. king
39. placed
40. with
41. possessions
42. and
43. his
44. the
45. to
46. in
47. the
48. and
49. the
50. great

Cloze Passage Coding Form and Answer Keys

## FORM 10B

1. brightly
2. as
3. among
4. and
5. the
6. and
7. alone
8. in
9. was
10. had
11. rock
12. remembered
13. ago
14. friends
15. the
16. that
17. in
18. around
19. year
20. agreed
21. first
22. the
23. crew
24. equipment
25. pack
26. they
27. admiration
28. even
29. cheering
30. them
31. first
32. serious
33. that
34. highly
35. they
36. each
37. that
38. be
39. their
40. now
41. great
42. that
43. hire
44. wanted
45. their
46. enough
47. the
48. it
49. a
50. as

## FORM 10C

1. became
2. which
3. ropes
4. acts
5. coffins
6. prison
7. Houdini's
8. early
9. boy
10. in
11. Erik
12. name
13. a
14. he
15. after
16. in
17. shows
18. country
19. tours
20. of
21. persuaded
22. escapes
23. he
24. challenge
25. a
26. himself
27. a
28. wrapped
29. dropped
30. of
31. almost
32. the
33. free
34. magical
35. seemed
36. them
37. them
38. spiritualists
39. powers
40. to
41. their
42. on
43. feats
44. and
45. normal
46. on
47. his
48. perform
49. escape
50. to

1. they
2. at
3. a
4. found
5. not
6. such
7. city
8. a
9. but
10. to
11. and
12. the
13. shorten
14. city
15. the
16. them
17. of
18. picturesque
19. selling
20. the
21. found
22. deplorable
23. isolated
24. entire
25. in
26. outdoor
27. food
28. searched
29. marketplace
30. the
31. the
32. with
33. were
34. later
35. separating
36. after
37. tales
38. people
39. girls
40. that
41. Yugoslavia
42. charming
43. there
44. explained
45. had
46. a
47. caused
48. preparation
49. a
50. two

1. like
2. after
3. or
4. plan
5. need
6. to
7. who
8. continue
9. challenging
10. locating
11. a
12. securing
13. endeavor
14. and
15. employers
16. employee
17. common
18. in
19. suitable
20. the
21. newspaper
22. patience
23. enormous
24. the
25. a
26. pursuing
27. divided
28. will
29. positions
30. waste
31. for
32. qualified
33. vacancy
34. the
35. write
36. for
37. is
38. résumé
39. accurate
40. abilities
41. a
42. and
43. granted
44. interview
45. factor
46. time
47. employer
48. the
49. be
50. company

Cloze Passage Coding Form and Answer Keys

**FORM 11C**

1. that
2. than
3. these
4. is
5. desire
6. many
7. in
8. need
9. teens
10. popular
11. themselves
12. a
13. can
14. these
15. of
16. and
17. person
18. from
19. called
20. of
21. opinion
22. either
23. is
24. which
25. conceit
26. which
27. although
28. frustrating
29. from
30. can
31. by
32. boosted
33. are
34. and
35. quickly
36. possible
37. begin
38. this
39. set
40. so
41. in
42. a
43. meet
44. person
45. teens
46. the
47. becomes
48. people
49. grow
50. in

**FORM 12A**

1. be
2. exam
3. prevent
4. back
5. had
6. at
7. argument
8. conversation
9. Steve's
10. table
11. objections
12. he
13. to
14. year
15. travel
16. girl
17. believed
18. he
19. would
20. of
21. the
22. hours
23. concerned
24. might
25. relationship
26. if
27. generous
28. not
29. parents
30. Steve's
31. that
32. dwelled
33. a
34. friend
35. believed
36. would
37. by
38. worry
39. would
40. his
41. would
42. to
43. seemed
44. college
45. his
46. to
47. work
48. Steve's
49. to
50. of

**FORM 12B**

1. affects
2. abilities
3. it
4. assignments
5. tests
6. there
7. many
8. last
9. these
10. this
11. are
12. that
13. changed
14. eliminated
15. be
16. waiting
17. in
18. the
19. in
20. response
21. about
22. that
23. they
24. therefore
25. least
26. any
27. than
28. reading
29. for
30. who
31. often
32. severe
33. and
34. inhibit
35. the
36. will
37. his
38. deadlines
39. gets
40. has
41. deadlines
42. help
43. to
44. procrastination
45. deadlines
46. is
47. only
48. providing
49. to
50. be

**FORM 12C**

1. environment
2. commune
3. among
4. who
5. and
6. very
7. group
8. they
9. they
10. tranquility
11. even
12. leaves
13. they
14. from
15. be
16. in
17. they
18. sure
19. of
20. there
21. bearing
22. first
23. often
24. to
25. because
26. modern
27. the
28. many
29. occupied
30. much
31. their
32. stoves
33. standard
34. their
35. televisions
36. an
37. insistently
38. unspoiled
39. approximate
40. living
41. the
42. or
43. night
44. visiting
45. the
46. a
47. neighbors
48. are
49. might
50. of

Cloze Passage Coding Form and Answer Keys

# Graded Word Lists

♦♦♦♦♦♦♦♦♦♦♦♦♦♦♦♦♦

There are two lists of 20 words each for each grade level from preprimer through 12th grade. In all, there are 560 words selected from 4,170 words contained within 11 graded word lists. The 560 words were selected after eliminating duplicate words and words with conflicting grade placements within the 11 lists.

The two sets of graded word lists, being words in isolation, should not be viewed as a measure of comprehension. The lists may be used to estimate the grade level of the passage to be administered, to assess a reader's word recognition (sight vocabulary) and word identification abilities, and to gain an approximation of the reader's independent, instructional, and frustration reading levels.

The first broad use of the word lists includes the estimation of which passage to administer, the assessment of word recognition abilities, and the approximation of the reader's reading levels. Each of these may be derived from the same process of a timed presentation of the word lists. Begin with the highest list on which you believe the reader can recognize all of the words. Each word on the list should be presented separately and for only about one second.

To present each word separately, there are several methods from which you may choose. One method is to use two blank index cards or pieces of paper. The point where the two cards meet can be opened to show the word, closed after the one-second exposure, and moved down the list for the next exposure. Another method uses a window cut in an index card or piece of paper. The window is slid down the list to show each word or the blank spaces between words. With both of these methods, noting where the top or bottom of the card is in relation to a previous or forthcoming word, combined with a little practice, should allow you to have the test word in the opening or window. A third method is to copy each word onto a blank index card and use the cards as flash cards. Regardless of which of the methods you choose, you should have two copies of the words ready—one for the reader, and your copy for scoring the reader's performance. The reader's copy should be folded or masked so that only the words on the appropriate list will be visible. Before you present the list to the reader, tell the reader that he or she will have two or three seconds to say each word.

Scoring the timed presentation of the words involves six basic notations. The notations regarding the reader's performance are recorded on your copy of the list under the column labeled "Timed." A list of the eight scoring notations follows. It contains the six notations for the timed reading to which there have been added two more for use during the untimed presentation of the words missed during the timed presentation. To this list you should add any notations that you feel will help you in evaluating a reader's performance.

### Word List Scoring Notations

| | |
|---|---|
| *A | assisted, you said the word for the reader |
| C | correct pronunciation |
| **D | dialectal pronunciation, record the word as said by the reader |
| DK | don't know response |
| M | mispronunciation, record the word as said by the reader |
| O | omitted or skipped |
| *P | paused |
| S | self-corrected |

The grade level of the passage to be administered should be the same as the highest level word list the reader can pronounce with no less than 19 correct.

The approximation of the reader's reading levels may be based upon:

| Level | Number correct |
|---|---|
| Independent | 19–20 |
| Instructional | 15–18 |
| Frustration | 14 or less |

Once the frustration level has been reached, the presentation of the word lists should be stopped. This guideline may be disregarded if the reader expresses an interest in continuing.

The second broad use of the word lists facilitates an indication of the reader's word identification (analysis) abilities. This may be obtained by presenting in an untimed manner the words missed during the timed presentation. Once again, you will need the copies of the words for the reader and yourself. The words may be presented in the same manner as previously employed with the exception that there is no time limit for the exposure of the word. The notations of the reader's performance are those listed above and are recorded on your copy of the list under the column labeled "Untimed." You may wish to add your own notations to these, with the intention of indicating the strengths and weaknesses on the Patterns of Word Identification Sheet that follows; this summary sheet is intended to help you determine the instructional implications in developing a reader's word identification skills.

*The Assisted and Paused notations are to be used with the six other notations when scoring an untimed performance.

**A word scored as having been a dialectal pronunciation should *not* be counted as an error or incorrect response.

| PP | Timed | Untimed | P | Timed | Untimed |
|---|---|---|---|---|---|
| that | _____ | _____ | any | _____ | _____ |
| am | _____ | _____ | give | _____ | _____ |
| fast | _____ | _____ | matter | _____ | _____ |
| get | _____ | _____ | this | _____ | _____ |
| this | _____ | _____ | your | _____ | _____ |
| green | _____ | _____ | went | _____ | _____ |
| let | _____ | _____ | under | _____ | _____ |
| me | _____ | _____ | goat | _____ | _____ |
| it | _____ | _____ | one | _____ | _____ |
| father | _____ | _____ | should | _____ | _____ |
| dog | _____ | _____ | ready | _____ | _____ |
| away | _____ | _____ | other | _____ | _____ |
| here | _____ | _____ | house | _____ | _____ |
| if | _____ | _____ | into | _____ | _____ |
| car | _____ | _____ | bus | _____ | _____ |
| big | _____ | _____ | come | _____ | _____ |
| house | _____ | _____ | did | _____ | _____ |
| blue | _____ | _____ | farm | _____ | _____ |
| go | _____ | _____ | ask | _____ | _____ |
| have | _____ | _____ | now | _____ | _____ |

| PP | Timed | Untimed | P | Timed | Untimed |
|---|---|---|---|---|---|
| a | _____ | _____ | work | _____ | _____ |
| we | _____ | _____ | that | _____ | _____ |
| but | _____ | _____ | about | _____ | _____ |
| what | _____ | _____ | girl | _____ | _____ |
| did | _____ | _____ | man | _____ | _____ |
| stop | _____ | _____ | new | _____ | _____ |
| come | _____ | _____ | of | _____ | _____ |
| to | _____ | _____ | put | _____ | _____ |
| for | _____ | _____ | well | _____ | _____ |
| back | _____ | _____ | boat | _____ | _____ |
| one | _____ | _____ | are | _____ | _____ |
| she | _____ | _____ | make | _____ | _____ |
| no | _____ | _____ | would | _____ | _____ |
| in | _____ | _____ | ball | _____ | _____ |
| like | _____ | _____ | home | _____ | _____ |
| my | _____ | _____ | paint | _____ | _____ |
| work | _____ | _____ | show | _____ | _____ |
| do | _____ | _____ | baby | _____ | _____ |
| not | _____ | _____ | say | _____ | _____ |
| want | _____ | _____ | face | _____ | _____ |

| 1 | Timed | Untimed | 2 | Timed | Untimed |
|---|---|---|---|---|---|
| game | _____ | _____ | another | _____ | _____ |
| way | _____ | _____ | table | _____ | _____ |
| long | _____ | _____ | silver | _____ | _____ |
| back | _____ | _____ | breath | _____ | _____ |
| some | _____ | _____ | leave | _____ | _____ |
| never | _____ | _____ | enough | _____ | _____ |
| party | _____ | _____ | drink | _____ | _____ |
| over | _____ | _____ | always | _____ | _____ |
| picture | _____ | _____ | better | _____ | _____ |
| forget | _____ | _____ | clear | _____ | _____ |
| coat | _____ | _____ | great | _____ | _____ |
| met | _____ | _____ | happen | _____ | _____ |
| thing | _____ | _____ | nothing | _____ | _____ |
| why | _____ | _____ | silent | _____ | _____ |
| room | _____ | _____ | wave | _____ | _____ |
| them | _____ | _____ | pound | _____ | _____ |
| garden | _____ | _____ | mouse | _____ | _____ |
| could | _____ | _____ | near | _____ | _____ |
| baby | _____ | _____ | follow | _____ | _____ |
| along | _____ | _____ | balloon | _____ | _____ |

| 1 | Timed | Untimed | 2 | Timed | Untimed |
|---|---|---|---|---|---|
| hurry | _____ | _____ | myself | _____ | _____ |
| grow | _____ | _____ | off | _____ | _____ |
| rolled | _____ | _____ | queen | _____ | _____ |
| someone | _____ | _____ | reach | _____ | _____ |
| thought | _____ | _____ | shout | _____ | _____ |
| very | _____ | _____ | heavy | _____ | _____ |
| under | _____ | _____ | chair | _____ | _____ |
| wagon | _____ | _____ | bring | _____ | _____ |
| struck | _____ | _____ | anyone | _____ | _____ |
| found | _____ | _____ | country | _____ | _____ |
| once | _____ | _____ | poor | _____ | _____ |
| work | _____ | _____ | please | _____ | _____ |
| kind | _____ | _____ | suddenly | _____ | _____ |
| laugh | _____ | _____ | thought | _____ | _____ |
| street | _____ | _____ | yourself | _____ | _____ |
| basket | _____ | _____ | unhappy | _____ | _____ |
| cat | _____ | _____ | done | _____ | _____ |
| came | _____ | _____ | broke | _____ | _____ |
| love | _____ | _____ | mile | _____ | _____ |
| her | _____ | _____ | goose | _____ | _____ |

| 3 | Timed | Untimed | 4 | Timed | Untimed |
|---|---|---|---|---|---|
| drew | ———— | ———— | wrecked | ———— | ———— |
| crawl | ———— | ———— | underneath | ———— | ———— |
| hollow | ———— | ———— | vulture | ———— | ———— |
| spent | ———— | ———— | sleeve | ———— | ———— |
| royalty | ———— | ———— | holiday | ———— | ———— |
| hoof | ———— | ———— | courage | ———— | ———— |
| rule | ———— | ———— | forge | ———— | ———— |
| storm | ———— | ———— | served | ———— | ———— |
| straight | ———— | ———— | government | ———— | ———— |
| doctor | ———— | ———— | offend | ———— | ———— |
| buzz | ———— | ———— | coward | ———— | ———— |
| family | ———— | ———— | bandit | ———— | ———— |
| seven | ———— | ———— | afternoon | ———— | ———— |
| door | ———— | ———— | tremble | ———— | ———— |
| clean | ———— | ———— | whimper | ———— | ———— |
| wrong | ———— | ———— | urgent | ———— | ———— |
| visit | ———— | ———— | guilty | ———— | ———— |
| teeth | ———— | ———— | freeze | ———— | ———— |
| fault | ———— | ———— | predict | ———— | ———— |
| excuse | ———— | ———— | slumber | ———— | ———— |

| 3 | Timed | Untimed | 4 | Timed | Untimed |
|---|---|---|---|---|---|
| fellow | _____ | _____ | gaze | _____ | _____ |
| block | _____ | _____ | strand | _____ | _____ |
| allow | _____ | _____ | release | _____ | _____ |
| circus | _____ | _____ | perched | _____ | _____ |
| beach | _____ | _____ | opposite | _____ | _____ |
| teacher | _____ | _____ | greet | _____ | _____ |
| warm | _____ | _____ | heave | _____ | _____ |
| except | _____ | _____ | blushing | _____ | _____ |
| command | _____ | _____ | armor | _____ | _____ |
| wire | _____ | _____ | afford | _____ | _____ |
| shoot | _____ | _____ | human | _____ | _____ |
| hunger | _____ | _____ | receive | _____ | _____ |
| silence | _____ | _____ | solid | _____ | _____ |
| perform | _____ | _____ | invade | _____ | _____ |
| secret | _____ | _____ | relief | _____ | _____ |
| middle | _____ | _____ | serious | _____ | _____ |
| listen | _____ | _____ | machine | _____ | _____ |
| daddy | _____ | _____ | laughter | _____ | _____ |
| chewed | _____ | _____ | certainly | _____ | _____ |
| broom | _____ | _____ | digest | _____ | _____ |

| 5 | Timed | Untimed | 6 | Timed | Untimed |
|---|---|---|---|---|---|
| bridge | —— | —— | assembly | —— | —— |
| frantic | —— | —— | telescope | —— | —— |
| bore | —— | —— | technical | —— | —— |
| define | —— | —— | hesitate | —— | —— |
| wealthy | —— | —— | blister | —— | —— |
| vehicle | —— | —— | calm | —— | —— |
| marriage | —— | —— | appeal | —— | —— |
| indicate | —— | —— | original | —— | —— |
| jungle | —— | —— | phase | —— | —— |
| grim | —— | —— | dwelt | —— | —— |
| sullen | —— | —— | evidence | —— | —— |
| typical | —— | —— | falter | —— | —— |
| wrestle | —— | —— | spice | —— | —— |
| mask | —— | —— | rebellion | —— | —— |
| document | —— | —— | navigator | —— | —— |
| ticket | —— | —— | transport | —— | —— |
| detour | —— | —— | violet | —— | —— |
| microscope | —— | —— | width | —— | —— |
| frontier | —— | —— | burglar | —— | —— |
| yarn | —— | —— | ankle | —— | —— |

| 5 | Timed | Untimed | 6 | Timed | Untimed |
|---|---|---|---|---|---|
| peaceful | ———— | ———— | wretch | ———— | ———— |
| nation | ———— | ———— | barter | ———— | ———— |
| feature | ———— | ———— | necessary | ———— | ———— |
| distress | ———— | ———— | customers | ———— | ———— |
| champion | ———— | ———— | lens | ———— | ———— |
| ancestor | ———— | ———— | yearning | ———— | ———— |
| ignore | ———— | ———— | definite | ———— | ———— |
| silence | ———— | ———— | exaggerate | ———— | ———— |
| taxation | ———— | ———— | flourish | ———— | ———— |
| military | ———— | ———— | tributary | ———— | ———— |
| catalog | ———— | ———— | admitting | ———— | ———— |
| impulse | ———— | ———— | graceful | ———— | ———— |
| summit | ———— | ———— | solemn | ———— | ———— |
| ornament | ———— | ———— | interval | ———— | ———— |
| develop | ———— | ———— | bail | ———— | ———— |
| considered | ———— | ———— | furiously | ———— | ———— |
| jagged | ———— | ———— | violent | ———— | ———— |
| wailing | ———— | ———— | initiation | ———— | ———— |
| custom | ———— | ———— | blond | ———— | ———— |
| husky | ———— | ———— | gorge | ———— | ———— |

| 7 | Timed | Untimed | 8 | Timed | Untimed |
|---|---|---|---|---|---|
| condescend | ———— | ———— | imperative | ———— | ———— |
| impetuous | ———— | ———— | restraint | ———— | ———— |
| violence | ———— | ———— | intrigue | ———— | ———— |
| peculiar | ———— | ———— | asphalt | ———— | ———— |
| dominion | ———— | ———— | breakthrough | ———— | ———— |
| neutral | ———— | ———— | intrigue | ———— | ———— |
| obvious | ———— | ———— | surgical | ———— | ———— |
| render | ———— | ———— | ransom | ———— | ———— |
| remarkable | ———— | ———— | induction | ———— | ———— |
| abject | ———— | ———— | ardent | ———— | ———— |
| fluency | ———— | ———— | certify | ———— | ———— |
| sculpture | ———— | ———— | justify | ———— | ———— |
| sundry | ———— | ———— | twilight | ———— | ———— |
| brilliant | ———— | ———— | whimpered | ———— | ———— |
| hurdle | ———— | ———— | naturalize | ———— | ———— |
| institution | ———— | ———— | entangled | ———— | ———— |
| unexplored | ———— | ———— | prolong | ———— | ———— |
| blight | ———— | ———— | figurative | ———— | ———— |
| immediately | ———— | ———— | gadget | ———— | ———— |
| attentively | ———— | ———— | philosophical | ———— | ———— |

| 7 | Timed | Untimed | 8 | Timed | Untimed |
|---|---|---|---|---|---|
| triumphant | ———— | ———— | barometer | ———— | ———— |
| lingering | ———— | ———— | delusion | ———— | ———— |
| confidential | ———— | ———— | memorandum | ———— | ———— |
| wrest | ———— | ———— | evident | ———— | ———— |
| caboose | ———— | ———— | crag | ———— | ———— |
| inquiry | ———— | ———— | tarnish | ———— | ———— |
| arsenal | ———— | ———— | psychology | ———— | ———— |
| gaseous | ———— | ———— | aloof | ———— | ———— |
| society | ———— | ———— | hearsay | ———— | ———— |
| fickle | ———— | ———— | sportsmanship | ———— | ———— |
| tenor | ———— | ———— | juvenile | ———— | ———— |
| vetoed | ———— | ———— | virtue | ———— | ———— |
| menace | ———— | ———— | universal | ———— | ———— |
| displease | ———— | ———— | dorsal | ———— | ———— |
| enlarge | ———— | ———— | edible | ———— | ———— |
| quench | ———— | ———— | faulty | ———— | ———— |
| perpetual | ———— | ———— | pretext | ———— | ———— |
| complexion | ———— | ———— | obsolete | ———— | ———— |
| observation | ———— | ———— | limitation | ———— | ———— |
| astronomer | ———— | ———— | circulation | ———— | ———— |

Graded Word Lists

| 9 | Timed | Untimed | 10 | Timed | Untimed |
|---|---|---|---|---|---|
| prestige | —— | —— | amnesty | —— | —— |
| vulnerable | —— | —— | irony | —— | —— |
| malicious | —— | —— | reputable | —— | —— |
| ecstasy | —— | —— | vigilant | —— | —— |
| defensive | —— | —— | crypt | —— | —— |
| creation | —— | —— | bereaved | —— | —— |
| legitimate | —— | —— | grotesque | —— | —— |
| urchin | —— | —— | phenomenal | —— | —— |
| scrutinize | —— | —— | fictitious | —— | —— |
| aggressive | —— | —— | oratory | —— | —— |
| judicial | —— | —— | tier | —— | —— |
| brazen | —— | —— | legacy | —— | —— |
| molecule | —— | —— | callous | —— | —— |
| precaution | —— | —— | artisan | —— | —— |
| gist | —— | —— | jerkin | —— | —— |
| ornate | —— | —— | inept | —— | —— |
| apparatus | —— | —— | annihilate | —— | —— |
| inventive | —— | —— | bevy | —— | —— |
| porous | —— | —— | tumult | —— | —— |
| glorify | —— | —— | secluded | —— | —— |

| 9 | Timed | Untimed | 10 | Timed | Untimed |
|---|---|---|---|---|---|
| disorganized | ———— | ———— | superlative | ———— | ———— |
| liaison | ———— | ———— | atrocious | ———— | ———— |
| suffice | ———— | ———— | barometer | ———— | ———— |
| technique | ———— | ———— | mire | ———— | ———— |
| memorable | ———— | ———— | devastate | ———— | ———— |
| disconsolate | ———— | ———— | glutton | ———— | ———— |
| consecutive | ———— | ———— | opaque | ———— | ———— |
| loiter | ———— | ———— | exuberant | ———— | ———— |
| sluggish | ———— | ———— | dirge | ———— | ———— |
| priority | ———— | ———— | marital | ———— | ———— |
| heathen | ———— | ———— | naive | ———— | ———— |
| gild | ———— | ———— | fallacy | ———— | ———— |
| pewter | ———— | ———— | negotiate | ———— | ———— |
| wane | ———— | ———— | ensemble | ———— | ———— |
| originate | ———— | ———— | foible | ———— | ———— |
| enviable | ———— | ———— | gender | ———— | ———— |
| obsolete | ———— | ———— | nausea | ———— | ———— |
| entice | ———— | ———— | eccentric | ———— | ———— |
| pungent | ———— | ———— | eloquent | ———— | ———— |
| grotesque | ———— | ———— | gratuitous | ———— | ———— |

| 11 | Timed | Untimed | 12 | Timed | Untimed |
|---|---|---|---|---|---|
| knoll | | | pedagogy | | |
| awry | | | zealous | | |
| philosophy | | | astringent | | |
| impediment | | | juncture | | |
| gauntlet | | | utilitarian | | |
| physiology | | | ignominious | | |
| virtuoso | | | bourgeois | | |
| waiver | | | obtuse | | |
| bequeath | | | wreak | | |
| retribution | | | facsimile | | |
| synchronize | | | staid | | |
| malign | | | inveigle | | |
| covet | | | veritable | | |
| deplete | | | defray | | |
| galore | | | colloquial | | |
| nutritious | | | lieu | | |
| tryst | | | quiescent | | |
| superannuate | | | vacillate | | |
| luxuriant | | | notoriety | | |
| assimilate | | | heresy | | |

| 11 | Timed | Untimed | 12 | Timed | Untimed |
|---|---|---|---|---|---|
| envisage | _____ | _____ | dissident | _____ | _____ |
| contraband | _____ | _____ | forensic | _____ | _____ |
| archaic | _____ | _____ | noxious | _____ | _____ |
| chastisement | _____ | _____ | polyglot | _____ | _____ |
| compressible | _____ | _____ | excruciating | _____ | _____ |
| whimsical | _____ | _____ | credence | _____ | _____ |
| elegy | _____ | _____ | bucolic | _____ | _____ |
| galore | _____ | _____ | hierarchy | _____ | _____ |
| risible | _____ | _____ | montage | _____ | _____ |
| aperture | _____ | _____ | syllogism | _____ | _____ |
| impediment | _____ | _____ | neophyte | _____ | _____ |
| malign | _____ | _____ | vascular | _____ | _____ |
| celestial | _____ | _____ | erudite | _____ | _____ |
| rotunda | _____ | _____ | caterwaul | _____ | _____ |
| crunch | _____ | _____ | plethora | _____ | _____ |
| epitaph | _____ | _____ | succinct | _____ | _____ |
| tryst | _____ | _____ | variegated | _____ | _____ |
| retribution | _____ | _____ | loquacious | _____ | _____ |
| swathe | _____ | _____ | garrulous | _____ | _____ |
| claimant | _____ | _____ | fallible | _____ | _____ |

Student _____

Indicate apparent consistent strengths (+) and weaknesses (−).

PATTERNS
OF WORD
IDENTIFI-
CATION

*De Santi
Cloze Reading
Inventory*

_____ assistance

_____ dialectal pronunciation

_____ don't know response

_____ mispronunciation

_____ omitted or skipped

_____ pauses

_____ self-correction

_____ word beginnings

_____ word middles

_____ word endings

_____ prefixes

_____ suffixes

_____ inflectional endings

_____ single consonants

_____ consonant clusters

_____ long vowels

_____ short vowels

_____ vowel digraphs

_____ diphthongs

_____ syllabication

_____ blending

_____ letter-by-letter sounding

_____ attempts only first letter

Instructional implications:

# Summary Sheets

◆◆◆◆◆◆◆◆◆◆◆◆◆◆◆

# INDIVIDUAL STUDENT RECORD SHEET

STUDENT _____ SEX M F GRADE _____ BIRTHDATE _____

TEACHER _____ ADMINISTERED BY _____ SCHOOL _____

TEST DATE _____

**De Santi Cloze Reading Inventory**

| Grade | Word lists: Number correct timed and untimed combined | Forms used | | Passages (Total percent for each) | | | |
|---|---|---|---|---|---|---|---|
| | | | | Traditional | Total | Logical language usage | Structure of language |
| PP | | | | | | | |
| P | | | | | | | |
| 1 | | | | | | | |
| 2 | | | | | | | |
| 3 | | | | | | | |
| 4 | | | | | | | |
| 5 | | | | | | | |
| 6 | | | | | | | |
| 7 | | | | | | | |
| 8 | | | | | | | |
| 9 | | | | | | | |
| 10 | | | | | | | |
| 11 | | | | | | | |
| 12 | | | | | | | |

| Estimated levels | | | | |
|---|---|---|---|---|
| | Words | | Passages | |
| Highest level with 19 or 20 correct | | Independent | | Highest passage with 58% or more |
| 15–18 correct | | Instructional | | 44–56% |
| 14 or fewer correct | | Frustration | | 42% or less |

Assigned Instructional Level _____

# CLASS SUMMARY SHEET OF GRADE LEVELS
*De Santi Cloze Reading Inventory*

| Student | Date | Words | | | | Passages | | | | | |
| | | Independent | Instructional | Frustration | | Independent | | Instructional | | Frustration | |
| | | | | | | Trad | Total | Trad | Total | Trad | Total |
|---|---|---|---|---|---|---|---|---|---|---|---|
| | | | | | | | | | | | |
| | | | | | | | | | | | |
| | | | | | | | | | | | |
| | | | | | | | | | | | |
| | | | | | | | | | | | |
| | | | | | | | | | | | |
| | | | | | | | | | | | |
| | | | | | | | | | | | |
| | | | | | | | | | | | |
| | | | | | | | | | | | |
| | | | | | | | | | | | |
| | | | | | | | | | | | |
| | | | | | | | | | | | |
| | | | | | | | | | | | |

**SUMMARY OF INSTRUCTIONAL GROUPS**

*De Santi*
*Cloze Reading*
*Inventory*

TEACHER ——————— CLASS ——————— DATE ———————

TEACHER ——————— CLASS ——————— DATE ———————

Group I                                    Group II

Group III                                  Group IV

# Technical Information

◆◆◆◆◆◆◆◆◆◆◆◆◆◆◆◆◆◆◆◆◆◆◆

This section includes the technical information pertinent to the development and testing of the inventory. Included are the passage (a) development guidelines, (b) readability and grammar estimates, and (c) appeal ratings. The section concludes with information on the validity and reliability of the inventory.

The inventory's passages were designed commensurate with traditional Cloze test construction guidelines. Each passage contains approximately 275 words with 50 deletions that are of standard length and numbered consecutively. The first and last sentences of each passage were left intact, with no deletions. The passages were the original writings of graduate level students enrolled in a reading specialist certification program and of undergraduate preservice reading education majors. These writings were subsequently modified and rewritten to meet the passage selection criteria that were employed.

The readability level of each passage was initially established using an extension of the Harris-Jacobson (1980) readability formula. Each passage was then double-checked using the Fry (1977) readability formula. Both the Harris-Jacobson and the Fry use sentence length and vocabulary difficulty to determine readability, although the Harris-Jacobson uses the number of words not on a given list, and the Fry uses the average number of syllables per word as measures of vocabulary difficulty. Only those passages that were determined to be at the appropriate grade levels by both formulas were considered for further scrutiny. This selection process was used to avoid the need to adapt passages to meet specific readability levels, since the use of formulas is not recommended with anything but "honestly" written text, that is, text that has been written without regard for satisfying readability levels (Bruce et al., 1981).

Passage selection criteria included comparisons of the syntactic complexity of the passages. Comparisons were made by counting the number of sentences, t-units, the average number of words, and embeddings per t-unit

(DeStefano, 1978; Hunt, 1965). The results of these comparisons are presented in Table 1.

The third set of passage selection criteria included rating the interest level and appeal of each passage. Initial selection was based on ratings by a professor of reading, a reading specialist with elementary and secondary experience, and a college level reading lab instructor. These raters used an interest checklist by grade level that was assembled from the literature (Stevens, 1981; Sheperd, 1973; Ashley, 1970; Meisel and Glass, 1970; King, 1967; Novell, 1958). The checklist included only general topics that received high appeal ratings from both boys and girls. The interest and appeal of each passage was then rated by the children included in the field testing of the inventory. The characteristics of this group are described below. Using a scale of 1, very interesting, through 3, not interesting, the mean ratings ranged from 1.26 to 1.98. The specific and mean ratings of each passage are presented in Table 2.

Finally, passage selection criteria also provided for the exclusion of any passage that contained conversation because of its tendency to have a subtle effect on a passage's readability (Helm, 1973). Both the expository and narrative styles were included because students are expected to read and learn from both styles. The inclusion of both styles had no apparent effect on the validity and reliability analyses that are reported below.

**Table 1**  *Passage Syntactic Complexity by T-Units and Embeddings*

| Grade | Form | Number of sentences | Number of t-units | Number of words per t-unit | Number of embeddings per t-unit |
|---|---|---|---|---|---|
| 3 | A | 27 | 30 | 9.17 | 1.15 |
|   | B | 26 | 30 | 9.50 | 1.60 |
|   | C | 25 | 28 | 10.03 | 1.30 |
| 4 | A | 20 | 20 | 14.3 | 1.8 |
|   | B | 17 | 17 | 16.2 | 2.3 |
|   | C | 29 | 30 | 9.4 | 2.0 |
| 5 | A | 23 | 23 | 11.82 | 2.39 |
|   | B | 22 | 22 | 12.77 | 1.95 |
|   | C | 20 | 27 | 10.59 | 2.00 |
| 6 | A | 22 | 22 | 12.8 | 2.5 |
|   | B | 17 | 23 | 12.0 | 2.9 |
|   | C | 19 | 19 | 14.5 | 2.7 |
| 7 | A | 17 | 19 | 15.37 | 2.84 |
|   | B | 19 | 20 | 13.90 | 2.55 |
|   | C | 20 | 21 | 14.24 | 2.43 |
| 8 | A | 14 | 16 | 19.1 | 3.6 |
|   | B | 19 | 19 | 14.7 | 3.2 |
|   | C | 17 | 20 | 14.4 | 2.7 |
| 9 | A | 17 | 19 | 15.58 | 3.47 |
|   | B | 16 | 19 | 15.73 | 3.32 |
|   | C | 14 | 16 | 18.50 | 3.06 |
| 10 | A | 16 | 18 | 15.9 | 3.7 |
|   | B | 16 | 16 | 18.9 | 3.7 |
|   | C | 16 | 16 | 17.6 | 4.5 |
| 11 | A | 15 | 15 | 18.60 | 4.26 |
|   | B | 16 | 16 | 17.75 | 3.50 |
|   | C | 17 | 18 | 16.89 | 3.61 |
| 12 | A | 12 | 13 | 22.0 | 3.8 |
|   | B | 16 | 16 | 18.1 | 3.5 |
|   | C | 14 | 16 | 17.1 | 4.1 |

Passage Interest Ratings with Percentages Given for Each of Three Ratings  **Table 2**
Including: 1 Very Interesting, 2 Fairly Interesting, and 3 Not Interesting

| | | Passage form | | | | | | | | |
| | | A | | | B | | | C | | |
| Grade | Rating | 1 | 2 | 3 | 1 | 2 | 3 | 1 | 2 | 3 |
|---|---|---|---|---|---|---|---|---|---|---|
| 3 | | 62 | 28 | 10 | 60 | 17 | 23 | 66 | 26 | 8 |
| | | | 1.48[a] | | | 1.64 | | | 1.42 | |
| 4 | | 48 | 28 | 23 | 48 | 32 | 20 | 46 | 26 | 28 |
| | | | 1.73 | | | 1.72 | | | 1.86 | |
| 5 | | 38 | 27 | 35 | 48 | 31 | 21 | 51 | 32 | 17 |
| | | | 1.97 | | | 1.73 | | | 1.49 | |
| 6 | | 53 | 32 | 15 | 64 | 26 | 10 | 37 | 28 | 35 |
| | | | 1.62 | | | 1.46 | | | 1.98 | |
| 7 | | 76 | 23 | 1 | 76 | 21 | 4 | 51 | 36 | 14 |
| | | | 1.26 | | | 1.28 | | | 1.63 | |
| 8 | | 61 | 30 | 9 | 36 | 42 | 22 | 65 | 23 | 12 |
| | | | 1.48 | | | 1.86 | | | 1.27 | |
| 9 | | 77 | 19 | 4 | 57 | 34 | 9 | 32 | 52 | 16 |
| | | | 1.26 | | | 1.52 | | | 1.85 | |
| 10 | | 47 | 42 | 10 | 44 | 41 | 15 | 65 | 22 | 13 |
| | | | 1.61 | | | 1.71 | | | 1.48 | |
| 11 | | 36 | 43 | 21 | 51 | 37 | 12 | 58 | 29 | 13 |
| | | | 1.85 | | | 1.61 | | | 1.54 | |
| 12 | | 50 | 45 | 3 | 41 | 32 | 27 | 41 | 44 | 15 |
| | | | 1.49 | | | 1.86 | | | 1.74 | |

a = Mean Interest Score
Mathematical discrepancies are due to rounding

The inventory was field tested 3,456 times with a total of 864 students drawn from two school systems. The first was a large urban public school system from which 456 students representing grades 3, 5, 7, 9, and 11 were drawn from four elementary, three junior, and three senior high schools. The second was a large suburban public school system from which 408 students representing grades 4, 6, 8, 10, and 12 were drawn from three elementary, three junior, and three senior high schools. Table 3 represents the number of participants by grade, sex, and race.

Number of Subjects by Grade, Sex, and Race  **Table 3**

| | Sex | | Race | | | |
| Grade | Female | Male | Black | White | Other | Totals |
|---|---|---|---|---|---|---|
| 3 | 45 | 44 | 42 | 46 | 1 | 89 |
| 4 | 48 | 36 | 5 | 77 | 2 | 84 |
| 5 | 54 | 48 | 58 | 43 | 1 | 102 |
| 6 | 43 | 45 | 5 | 81 | 2 | 88 |
| 7 | 54 | 48 | 62 | 34 | 6 | 102 |
| 8 | 42 | 53 | 17 | 70 | 8 | 95 |
| 9 | 41 | 46 | 67 | 19 | 1 | 87 |
| 10 | 36 | 40 | 10 | 57 | 9 | 76 |
| 11 | 36 | 40 | 46 | 28 | 2 | 76 |
| 12 | 35 | 30 | 2 | 62 | 1 | 65 |
| Totals | 434 | 430 | 314 | 517 | 33 | 864 |

In addition to demographic information, two sets of data were collected regarding each student. The first set included performance on each of the Cloze passages at a student's grade level. The second set included the student's vocabulary, comprehension, and total reading scores on the Comprehensive Test of Basic Skills (CTBS), which is regularly administered by each of the school systems. These data were used in the validity and reliability calculations.

Both concurrent and predictive validity were determined by calculating Pearson product-moment correlations between the inventory's four interpretive values (Traditional Comprehension, Total Comprehension, Logical Language Usage, Grammatical Awareness) and the three CTBS scores (vocabulary, comprehension, total reading) for each of the three passage. One hundred eighty correlations (4 values × 3 scores × 3 passages × 5 grades = 180) were analyzed for concurrent validity. Because the 12th grade (65 subjects) graduated from high school between the first and second administrations of the CTBS, this grade level was not included in the predictive validity analysis. As a result, 144 correlations (4 values × 3 scores × 3 passages × 4 grades = 144) were analyzed to estimate predictive validity.

Given the impracticability of presenting the 324 correlations within the confines of this section, the results of the data analyses are presented as frequency distributions of the level of statistical significance for each of the correlations. Table 4 reports the statistical significance of the 180 concurrent validity correlations. It is organized according to inventory interpretative value, grade, passage, CTBS score, and level of significance. One hundred fifty (83.3%) of the correlations were significant at the .001 level, 24 (13.3%) at the .01 level, and 6 (3.3%) at the .05 level. All 180 correlations were significant at at least the .05 level. Table 5 reports the statistical significance of the 144 predictive validity correlations and follows the same organizational format as Table 4. One hundred two (70.8%) of the correlations were significant at the .001 level, 23 (16%) at the .01 level, 9 (6.3%) at the .05 level, and 10 (6.9%) were not significant. One

***Table 4*** *Statistical Significance of 180 Concurrent Validity Correlations: DCRI Interpretive Values by Grade Level, Passage, and CTBS Scores*

| | CRI interpretive values | | | | | | | | | | | | | | | | | | | |
| | *Traditional* | | | | | *Total* | | | | | *Logical Language* | | | | | *Grammatical Awareness* | | | | |
| *Grade* | *4* | *6* | *8* | *10* | *12* | *4* | *6* | *8* | *10* | *12* | *4* | *6* | *8* | *10* | *12* | *4* | *6* | *8* | *10* | *12* |
| **Voc.** | | | | | | | | | | | | | | | | | | | | |
| 1 | bc | abc | abc | abc | abc | c | abc | ac | abc | abc | bc | abc | ab | abc | abc | bc | b | abc | | abc |
| 2 | a | | | | | | | ab | | b | | | | c | | a | | c | | abc |
| 3 | | | | | | | | | | | | | a | | | | | a | | |
| **Comp.** | | | | | | | | | | | | | | | | | | | | |
| 1 | abc | abc | ab | abc | ac | ac | abc | a | abc | abc | c | abc | ab | abc | ac | abc | abc | ab | | ac |
| 2 | | | c | | | | | b | b | c | | ab | | | | | | c | ac | b |
| 3 | | | | | | | | b | | | | | c | b | | | | | b | |
| **Tot.** | | | | | | | | | | | | | | | | | | | | |
| 1 | abc | abc | abc | abc | abc | abc | abc | abc | abc | abc | bc | abc | abc | abc | abc | abc | abc | abc | | abc |
| 2 | | | | | | | | | a | | | | | | | | | | | abc |
| 3 | | | | | | | | | | | | | | | | | | | | |

1 = $p$ or = .001          a = first passage within grade level
2 = $p$ = .002 through .01     b = second passage within grade level
3 = $p$ = .011 through .05     c = third passage within grade level

    Technical Information

hundred thirty-four of the 144 correlations (93%) were significant at at least the .05 level. When combined across both validity analyses, the 324 correlations were distributed as: 252 (77.8%) significant at the .001 level, 47 (14.5%) at the .01 level, 15 (4.6%) at the .05 level, and 10 (3%) not significant. Three hundred fourteen of the 324 correlations (97%) were significant at at least the .05 level.

To establish the equivalence of forms, the strength of association between students' performance on the various passages at each grade level were established through the calculation of Omega Squared values. Of the 80 values calculated with the data from the suburban sample, 72 were below .10 with 78 being below .20. Cooney and Zinkgraf (1979) state that Omega Squared values of approximately .20 are considered quite low, and Halderson and Glasnapp (1972) suggest that values of .10 or less can be considered of no practical significance. As a result, there is little or no practical significance in the differences observed in students' performances on the passages within each grade level, and they may be used interchangeably.

The average alternate forms reliability coefficient for grades 3 through 12 was found to be .61. As a result, users of the inventory can be fairly certain that the use of alternate forms will yield similar estimates of students' reading proficiency.

Single-rater reliabilities were calculated to determine if a variety of teachers could consistently score students' performances on a variety of passages. From the urban sample, 10 students were randomly selected from each of the five grade levels. The 150 passages of these 50 students were randomly assigned and scored by a group of seven raters using the scoring directions. Each of the seven raters had a minimum of five years teaching experience, was either from the elementary or secondary level, and was a student in a graduate level

*Statistical Significance of 144 Predictive Validity Correlations:*    *Table 5*
*DCRI Interpretative Values by Grade Level, Passage, and CTBS Scores*

CRI interpretative values

| Grade | Traditional | | | | Total | | | | Logical Language | | | | Grammatical Awareness | | | |
|---|---|---|---|---|---|---|---|---|---|---|---|---|---|---|---|---|
|  | 4 | 6 | 8 | 10 | 4 | 6 | 8 | 10 | 4 | 6 | 8 | 10 | 4 | 6 | 8 | 10 |
| **Voc.** | | | | | | | | | | | | | | | | |
| 1 | abc | abc | abc | abc | bc | abc | ac | bc | ab | abc | abc | b | ab | c | ab | b |
| 2 |  |  |  |  |  |  | a |  |  |  |  | a |  | b | c | ac |
| 3 |  |  |  |  | a |  |  |  | c |  |  |  |  |  |  |  |
| 4 |  |  |  |  |  |  | b |  |  |  |  | c | c | a |  |  |
| **Comp.** | | | | | | | | | | | | | | | | |
| 1 | bc | abc | abc | abc | c | abc | ac | abc |  | abc | a | b | b | bc | ab |  |
| 2 | a |  |  |  |  |  |  |  | bc |  | b | a | a |  | c | abc |
| 3 |  |  |  |  |  |  |  |  |  |  | c | c | c | a |  |  |
| 4 |  |  |  |  | ab |  | b |  | a |  |  |  |  |  |  |  |
| **Tot.** | | | | | | | | | | | | | | | | |
| 1 | abc | abc | abc | abc | c | abc | ac | abc | b | abc | ab | b | ac | bc | ab | bc |
| 2 |  |  |  |  | a |  |  |  | ac |  | c | a |  |  | c | a |
| 3 |  |  |  |  | b |  |  |  |  |  |  | c | b |  |  |  |
| 4 |  |  |  |  |  |  | b |  |  |  |  |  |  | a |  |  |

1 = p ˌor = .001                a = first passage within grade level
2 = p = .002 through .01        b = second passage within grade level
3 = p = .011 through .05        c = third passage within grade level
4 = p ˝ .05

reading specialist program. Averaged across forms and grade levels, the mean reliabilities for single-raters for the interpretative values of Traditional Comprehension, Total Comprehension, Logical Language Usage, and Grammatical Awareness were .95, .81, .86, and .58. Following these results, the instructions for the Grammatical Awareness value were refined and Sample Codings were developed to increase reliability (De Santi and Sullivan, 1985).

Inter-rater reliabilities were calculated to determine if different raters could consistently rate students' performances. The passages and the raters were the same as those described under single-rater reliability. Each passage was rated by three of the raters for a total of 450 passages. Averaged across forms and grade levels, the mean reliabilities for inter-rating the interpretative values of Traditional Comprehension, Total Comprehension, Logical Language Usage, and Grammatical Awareness were .97, .93, .96, and .75 (De Santi and Sullivan, 1984).

The scale for identifying a reader's independent, instructional, and frustration reading levels from the Total Comprehension interpretative value was determined through a discriminant function analysis based on the range of scores from the Traditional Comprehension interpretative values.

# References

♦♦♦♦♦♦♦

Ashley, L. F. (1970). Children's reading interests and individualized reading. *Elementary English, 47,* 1088–1096.

Bruce, B. C. (1981). Plans and social actions. In R. J. Spiro, B. C. Bruce, and W. F. Brewer (Eds), *Theoretical issues in reading comprehension.* Hillsdale, New Jersey: Lawrence Erlbaum Associates.

Cooney, J. and Zinkgraf, S. (1979). *Look beyond your F-test: Estimating statistical association in ANOVA models.* Paper presented at the Southwest Educational Research Association.

Cronbach, L. J. (1951). Coefficient alpha and the internal structure of tests. *Psychometrika, 16,* 297–334.

De Santi, R. J. and Sullivan, V. G. (1984). Inter-rater reliability of the cloze reading inventory as a qualitative measure of reading comprehension. *Reading Psychology: An International Quarterly, 5,* 203–208.

De Santi, R. J. and Sullivan, V. G. (1985). Reliability of single-rater judgments of semantic and syntactic classifications of cloze test responses. *Journal of Research and Development in Education, 18,* 47–53.

DeStefano, J. S. (1978). *Language, the learner and the school.* New York: John Wiley and Sons.

Fry, E. (1977). Fry's readability graph: Clarifications, validity, and extension to level 17. *Journal of Reading, 21,* 242–252.

Halderson, I. and Glasnapp, D. (1972). Generalized rules for calculating the magnitude of an effect in factorial and repeated measures ANOVA designs. *American Educational Research Journal, 9,* 301–310.

Harris, A. J. and Jacobson, M. D. (1980). The Harris-Jacobson readability formula. In A. J. Harris and E. R. Sipay, *How to increase reading ability* (7th ed). New York: Longman.

Helm, E. B. (1973). Uses of the cloze procedure in elementary schools. In P. L. Nacke (Ed), *Programs and practices for college reading (Vol 2), 22nd Yearbook of the National Reading Conference.* Boone, North Carolina: National Reading Conference.

Hunt, K. (1965). *Grammatical structures written at three grade levels*. Champaign, Illinois: National Council of Teachers of English.

King, E. M. (1967). Critical appraisal of research on children's reading interests, preferences, and habits. *Canadian Education and Research Digest, 7,* 312–326.

Meisel, S. and Glass, G. G. (1970). Voluntary reading interests and the interest content of basal readers. *The Reading Teacher, 23,* 655–659.

Novell, G. W. (1958). *What boys and girls like to read*. Morristown, New Jersey: Silver Burdett Company.

Sheperd, D. L. (1973). *Comprehensive high school reading methods*. Columbus, Ohio: Charles E. Merrill.

Stevens, K. C. (1981). Reading interests among fifth and sixth graders. *The Reading Teacher, 21,* 147–151.

# Appendix: Scoring and Interpreting Exercises

◆◆◆◆◆◆◆◆◆◆◆◆◆◆◆◆◆◆◆◆◆◆◆◆◆◆

The materials in this appendix may be used to practice the scoring and interpretation of the DCRI as an in-class or take-home activity for university courses, for an in service meeting, or by individuals gaining competence with the inventory.

The appendix is divided into two parts. Part One includes a fourth grade and a tenth grade passage; each has been filled in by a student and is followed by a completely scored coding form and an interpretation of the results. To practice the scoring and interpretation of the DCRI, copy the coding form on pages 90–91 so that you can independently score and interpret the student's performance. Then compare your work with the scoring and interpretation provided.

Part Two of the appendix also includes a fourth and tenth grade passage, each of which is filled in by a student. These may be used for further scoring and interpreting practice and as a common basis for discussions regarding coding, scoring, and interpreting a particular reader's performance.

These are student-completed passages and their backup documents. **PART ONE**

# Form 4B  The Amazing Circus

READER'S NAME ___John___

Going to the circus is fun. There are lots ___of___ interesting people and
                                            1
animals ___and___ tricks that are truly ___amazed___ .
         2                               3
   If you watch the ___lion___ tamer in the cage ___for___ several
                    4                             5
big cats at ___this___ time, it is thrilling. ___If___ you hear the
            6                                 7
tigers ___or___ lions roar, you wonder ___what___ they are ready to
       8                               9
___do___ their master. But soon ___he___ discover that the
10                               11
ferocious ___animals___ are just part of ___a___ show.
          12                             13
   You can see ___animals___ doing a variety of ___shows___ at the circus.
               14                               15
They ___sit___ on their hind paws ___they___ balance balls on their
     16                            17
___noses___ . We wish we could ___make___ our dogs to sit
18                              19
___down___ come upon our command.
20
   ___It___ is always amazing that ___the___ juggler can handle
   21                              22
so ___many___ balls or other objects ___over___ his hands at one
   23                                24
___time___ . But many jugglers even ___put___ their feet and head
25                                  26
___in___ their acts.
27
   The juggler ___throws___ to be quick, but ___a___ magician has to
               28                             29
be ___lots___ faster to fool the ___people___ . You can see elephants
   30                            31
___in___ cars disappear before your ___eyes___ . And no matter how
32                                  33
___hard___ you try you cannot ___find___ how these tricks are
34                             35
___done___ .
36

You might find yourself __*hold*__ your breath as you __*see*__
37                                          38
the acrobats flying through __*the*__ air from one swing __*over*__
39                                          40
the other. And it __*is*__ thrilling to watch the __*tight*__ rope
41                                          42
walker balance on __*his*__ narrow rope.
43

You can __*see*__ all the way through __*the*__ circus because
44                                          45
there are __*some*__ clowns nearby doing silly __*things*__. It is
46                                          47
surprising that __*one*__ are never hurt when __*they*__ hit each
48                                          49
other and __*stand*__ over their own big feet.
50

It is fun to see all of these entertaining people and animals at the circus.

| DN | Word deleted | Reader's choice | Blank | Exact | C&C | Sem | None | NGS |
|----|-------------|-----------------|-------|-------|-----|-----|------|-----|
| 1 | of | S (same) | | ✗ | | | | |
| 2 | doing | and | | | | ✗ | | |
| 3 | amazing | amazed | | ✗ | | | | ✗ |
| 4 | lion | S | | ✗ | | | | |
| 5 | with | for | | | | ✗ | | |
| 6 | a | this | | | | ✗ | | |
| 7 | When | If | | | | ✗ | | |
| 8 | and | or | | | ✗ | | | |
| 9 | if | what | | | | ✗ | | |
| 10 | attack | do | | | | ✗ | | ✗ |
| 11 | you | he | | | | ✗ | | ✗ |
| 12 | growls | animals | | | | ✗ | | |
| 13 | the | a | | | ✗ | | | |
| 14 | dogs | animals | | | | ✗ | | |
| 15 | tricks | shows | | | | ✗ | | |
| 16 | walk | sit | | | | ✗ | | |
| 17 | and | they | | | | ✗ | | ✗ |
| 18 | noses | S | | ✗ | | | | |
| 19 | teach | make | | | | ✗ | | ✗ |
| 20 | and | down | | | | | ✗ | |
| 21 | It | S | | ✗ | | | | |
| 22 | a | the | | | ✗ | | | |
| 23 | many | S | | ✗ | | | | |
| 24 | in | over | | | | ✗ | | |
| 25 | time | S | | ✗ | | | | |

| DN | Word deleted | Reader's choice | Blank | Exact | C&C | Sem | None | NGS |
|----|-------------|-----------------|-------|-------|-----|-----|------|-----|
| 26 | use | put | | | X | | | |
| 27 | in | S | | X | | | | |
| 28 | has | throws | | | | X | | |
| 29 | the | a | | | X | | | |
| 30 | even | lots | | | X | | | |
| 31 | audience | people | | | X | | | |
| 32 | and | in | | | | X | | |
| 33 | eyes | S | | X | | | | |
| 34 | hard | S | | X | | | | |
| 35 | see | find | | | X | | | |
| 36 | accomplished | done | | | X | | | |
| 37 | holding | hold | | X | | | | X |
| 38 | watch | see | | | X | | | |
| 39 | the | S | | X | | | | |
| 40 | to | over | | | | X | | |
| 41 | is | S | | X | | | | |
| 42 | tight | S | | X | | | | |
| 43 | the | his | | | X | | | |
| 44 | laugh | see | | | | X | | |
| 45 | the | S | | X | | | | |
| 46 | always | some | | | | X | | |
| 47 | stunts | things | | | | X | | |
| 48 | they | one | | | | X | | X |
| 49 | they | they | | X | | | | |
| 50 | fall | stand | | | | X | | |
| Total number | | | 0 | 16 | 11 | 22 | 1 | 7 |
| Total percent | | | 0 | 32 | 22 | 44 | 2 | 14 |

Traditional comprehension      32

Total comprehension      54

Logical language usage      98

Structure of language (100%—TP NGS)      86

## STRENGTHS

1. John shows a knowledge that the text must make sense as evidenced by no response being coded as None.
2. John's level of background knowledge and experience with circuses appears to be sufficient for comprehending the passage. This is evidenced by his knowledge of terms such as: lion tamer (#4), tight rope walker (#42), and by an awareness that jugglers have balls over (#24) their hands and that the juggler throws things (#28).

## WEAKNESSES

1. John has a tendency to overrely on experience and does not make use of many cues within the text that make responses based on experience alone incorrect (#24 and 28).
2. Inattention to syntax—numbers 3, 10, 11, 37, and 48.
3. Inattention to punctuation—to make sense, the response for number 17 requires a period before it.
4. Disregard of context across several sentences, of the story as a whole:
   Context of sentence—
   (a) Number 50 clowns cannot be *hurt* by *standing* over their big feet;
   (b) Number 28 juggler *throws* is a response based on what jugglers in general do, but is not related to the rest of the sentence; and
   (c) Number 20 sit *down* is a frequently used phrase, but it does not fit the context of the sentence.
   Context of total story—
   (a) Number 12 reading from the beginning of the paragraph, it is obvious that *animals* are part of the show but the use of *hind paws* should cue *dogs;* and
   (b) Number 13 *a* show implies that the animals are separate from what the audience is watching.
5. Imprecise use of vocabulary—number 15 *shows* rather than *tricks,* number 35 *find* for *see,* number 47 *things* for *stunts.*

*Interpretations of John's Performance on "The Amazing Circus"*

# Form 10A  The Amazing Pyramids

READER'S NAME ___*Mary*___

The Superdome and World Trade Center are both great feats of modern engineering. However, human beings have ___*been*___ building amazing structures for ___*hundreds*___ of
years, and when ___*they*___ stop to think about ___*what*___ limited technology
used to ___*make*___ some of these early ___*buildings*___, you may think they
___*built*___ even more amazing than ___*new*___ ones.

   The Egyptian pyramids ___*gave*___ examples of structures built ___*by*___
limited technology. Though the ___*foreign*___ Egyptians had only simple ___*houses*___
made of wood, stone, ___*mud*___ and brass, they were ___*supposed*___ to cut, move,
and ___*build*___ stones that weighed many ___*pounds*___ each in order to
___*build*___ their pyramids. These were ___*very*___ well-constructed that they
___*also*___ stand today.

   The pyramids ___*were*___ huge. They sit on ___*four*___ square bases and
have ___*a*___ smooth, triangular sides that ___*come*___ to a sharp point
___*at*___ the top. All were ___*made*___ by slaves, who worked
___*under*___ the direction of Egyptian ___*rulers*___. Many lives were lost
___*and*___ many people were badly ___*hurt*___ during the hundreds of
___*years*___ the pyramids were under ___*construction*___.

   The pyramids were built ___*to*___ house the dead bodies ___*of*___
Egyptian kings. The Egyptians ___*thought*___ that a person's soul ___*might*___ live
forever, as long ___*as*___ the body was cared ___*for*___. Therefore, when an
Egyptian ___*man*___ died, his body was ___*put*___ inside a pyramid, along
___*with*___ most of his valuable ___*things*___, a lot of food ___*and*___

drink, and sometimes even _____*his*_____ wife, family, and servants. _____*the*_____
43                                             44
pyramid was then sealed _____*to*_____ keep the king safe.
45

_____*After*_____ later times, many of _____*the*_____ pyramids were broken into
46                                      47
_____*or*_____ looted by robbers. But _____*many*_____ pyramids stand today as
48                                      49
_____*old*_____ monuments to the civilization that created them. They are just one example of
50
amazing structures created by ancient man.

**CLOZE
PASSAGE
CODING
FORM**

*De Santi
Cloze Reading
Inventory*

| DN | Word deleted | Reader's choice | Coding categories | | | | | |
|----|--------------|-----------------|-------|-------|-----|-----|------|-----|
| | | | Blank | Exact | C&C | Sem | None | NGS |
| 1 | been | S (same) | | X | | | | |
| 2 | hundreds | S | | X | | | | |
| 3 | you | they | | | | X | | |
| 4 | the | what | | | X | | | X |
| 5 | build | make | | | X | | | |
| 6 | structures | buildings | | | X | | | |
| 7 | are | built | | | | X | | X |
| 8 | modern | new | | | X | | | |
| 9 | are | gave | | | | | X | |
| 10 | with | by | | | | X | | |
| 11 | ancient | foreign | | | | X | | |
| 12 | tools | houses | | | | X | | |
| 13 | copper | mud | | | | X | | |
| 14 | able | supposed | | | | X | | |
| 15 | raise | build | | | | | X | |
| 16 | tons | pounds | | | | X | | |
| 17 | build | S | | X | | | | |
| 18 | so | very | | | X | | | X |
| 19 | still | also | | | X | | | |
| 20 | are | were | | X | | | | X |
| 21 | perfect | four | | | | X | | |
| 22 | four | a | | | | X | | X |
| 23 | rise | come | | | X | | | |
| 24 | at | S | | X | | | | |
| 25 | built | made | | | X | | | |

| DN | Word deleted | Reader's choice | Blank | Exact | C&C | Sem | None | NGS |
|----|----|----|----|----|----|----|----|----|
| | | | | Coding categories | | | | |
| 26 | under | S | | X | | | | |
| 27 | overseers | rulers | | | | X | | |
| 28 | and | S | | X | | | | |
| 29 | injured | hurt | | | X | | | |
| 30 | years | S | | X | | | | |
| 31 | construction | S | | X | | | | |
| 32 | to | S | | X | | | | |
| 33 | of | S | | X | | | | |
| 34 | believed | thought | | | X | | | |
| 35 | could | might | | | X | | | |
| 36 | as | S | | X | | | | |
| 37 | for | S | | X | | | | |
| 38 | king | man | | | | X | | |
| 39 | placed | put | | | X | | | |
| 40 | with | S | | X | | | | |
| 41 | possessions | things | | | X | | | |
| 42 | and | S | | X | | | | |
| 43 | his | S | | X | | | | |
| 44 | The | S | | X | | | | |
| 45 | to | S | | X | | | | |
| 46 | In | After | | | | X | | |
| 47 | the | S | | X | | | | |
| 48 | and | or | | | | X | | |
| 49 | the | many | | | | X | | |
| 50 | great | old | | | | X | | |
| Total number | | | 0 | 19 | 13 | 16 | 2 | 5 |
| Total percent | | | 0 | 38 | 26 | 32 | 4 | 10 |

Traditional comprehension   38

Total comprehension   64

Logical language usage   96

Structure of language (100%—TP NGS)   90

**WEAKNESSES**

1. Lack of technical vocabulary or use of simplistic language—number 5 *make* for *build*, number 6 *buildings* for *structures*, number 8 *new* for *modern*, number 25 *made* for *built*, number 29 *hurt* for *injuries*, number 41 *things* for *possessions*.
2. Syntax difficulties—number 3 *they* does not agree with *you* later in the sentence and seems to imply that people from hundreds of years ago now think..., number 4 "...about *what* limited technology used" creates a sentence with no verb, number 22 *a* smooth triangular sides—lacks number agreement.
3. Inattention to context—number 11 *foreign* Egyptians does not demonstrate awareness of time period, number 12 *houses* does not fit context of a paragraph about pyramids, number 16 *pounds* rather than *tons*, number 38 *man* rather than *king* ignores earlier information that pyramids were built to house bodies of kings.

*Interpretations of Mary's Performance on "The Amazing Pyramids"*

**PART TWO** These student-completed passages are for further exercise in scoring and interpreting the DCRI.

Appendix: Scoring and Interpreting Exercises

# Form 4C Reptiles

READER'S NAME _____

Reptiles are strange and beautiful animals. Reptiles __*are*__ bodies that
are covered __*over*__ small scales. Lizards and __*frogs*__ are
reptiles. Alligators, crocodiles, __*and*__ turtles are reptiles, too.
__*Alligators*__ have very long tails. __*If*__ an enemy grabs one
__*on*__ the tail, it snaps __*back*__. The lizard runs away.
__*then*__ it will grow a __*another*__ tail.
Snakes are interesting __*animals*__. Some snakes are harmless
__*and*__ cannot hurt you. Some __*snakes*__ are very poisonous. They
__*have*__ fangs which are like __*long*__, hollow teeth. When these
__*teeth*__ bite, the fangs fill __*up*__ poison which can kill
__*some*__ animals and people too.
__*sharks*__ catch fish in their __*huge*__ jaws. These reptiles
spend __*all*__ of their lives in __*warm*__ water. Most people have
__*to*__ telling the difference between __*a*__ alligator and
another reptile __*like*__ the crocodile. The alligator __*has*__ a
broad, fat snout __*it*__ likes swamps. The crocodile __*has*__ a
long, sharp snout.

__*An*__ interesting reptile is the __*turtle*__. All turtles hatch
from __*eggs*__. The mother turtle comes __*out*__ of the water to
__*put*__ her eggs on the __*beach*__. As soon as the __*baby*__

turtles hatch they hurry _____to_____ the beach to their _____water_____ in
                              36                                    37
the sea.

　　　Some _____animals_____ are small; others are _____very_____ large. Some
                    38                                    39
have scales _____with_____ bright colors and are _____fun_____ to see. Others
                  40                                    41
are _____ to see because they _____ their surroundings.
          42                                43
Some reptiles _____are_____ helpful to man. Some _____are_____ harmful to
                    44                                    45
man. If _____you_____ are not familiar with _____them_____ , you should visit
              46                                    47
your _____own_____ zoo. Reptiles are strange, _____scary_____ creatures. They
            48                                        49
are all _____part_____ of our world of nature. Studying about reptiles can be fun.
              50

# Form 10C  The Great Houdini

READER'S NAME _____

Simply reading or hearing the name, Houdini, brings to mind thoughts of magic and great

escapes. Years ago, Harry Houdini _was_ famous for performances in

_which_ he released himself from _chains_ and handcuffs. His challenging
1

_feets_ included freeing himself from _trunks_, straight jackets, and
2                                  3

various _types_ cells around the world.
4              5

_His_ stage career began very _early_ when, as a young
6

_man_ he performed acrobatic feats _with_ a circus, calling himself
7                              8

_Houdini_. Later he took the _Great_ Houdini in honor of _a_
9                      10                                      13
11                              12

famous magician for whom _he_ had great admiration.
14

Soon _after_ this, he began working _for_ dime museums and
15

vaudeville _theaters_, traveling all over the _country_. During one of these
16                                        17

_journeys_, he attracted the attention _of_ an influential producer who
18                                      19

_taught_ him to specialize in _magic_. His fame spread as
20                                21

_he_ perfected these and his _other_ acts.
22                              23

In response to _a_ challenge, he once allowed _himself_ to be
24                                    25

locked in _a_ trunk. This was then _bound_ in steel tape, and
26                                      27

_plunged_ into a river. Thousands _of_ spectators waited breathlessly for
28                                   29

_nearly_ a full minute until _the_ Great Houdini finally reappeared,
30                                    31                              32

_rid_ of his shackles.
33

As _incredible_ as Houdini's spectacular feats _appeared_ to those who
34                                            35

viewed _them_, he refused to describe _himself_ as supernatural. Claims by
36                                      37

_people_ that he had such _powers_ made him angry enough
38                                  39

_to_ publish an investigation of _his_ practices. Houdini prided
40                                      41

Copyright © 1986 by Allyn and Bacon, Inc. Use of this material is restricted to duplication from this master.

**Appendix: Scoring and Interpreting Exercises**       153

himself _____on_____ the fact that his _____tricks_____ could be logically explained
42 · 43
_____and_____ understood by anyone of _____moderate_____ intelligence.
44 · 45

Harry Houdini died _____on_____ Halloween night, after telling _____his_____
46 · 47
wife that he would _____perform_____ his greatest feat, an _____escape_____ from death, and
48 · 49
return _____to_____ her on an anniversary of his demise. Unfortunately, he never managed
50
to perfect that act.